Matthew D. Skirton
Missionary, Me?

Matthew D. Skirton

Missionary, Me?

Bibliographic information published by the Deutsche Nationalbibliothek
The Deutsche Nationalbibliothek lists this publication in the Deutsche
Nationalbibliografie;
detailed bibliographic data are available in the Internet at http://dnb.d-nb.de.

© 2015 OM Books
Alte Neckarelzer Straße 2 · 74821 Mosbach · Deutschland
www.d.om.org
ISBN 978-3-902669-21-6

First published February 2015
3rd revised printing June 2018
Cover Design: Kiet Van
Layout: Heike Schneider · Wetzlar/Germany

Matthew.MissionaryMe@gmail.com
For more information or to order copies of this book visit Facebook Missionary, Me?
For more information about OM International visit www.om.org (/Moldova)

*This book is dedicated to the girl who inspired and challenged
me to really know God; Helen, my wife and best friend.
It has been some journey so far!*

*And to my children Hanna, Lydia, Rachel, David and James;
you make life joyful and fun and I am so thankful
you are sharing this journey with us.*

EUROPE

MOLDOVA

Contents

Acknowledgements

As I have taken time to reflect upon my life and write out my story I realise that there have been so many people who have 'leant in' and helped Helen and me over the years. I thank especially Thomas Bucher, Hamilton Adams and Dennis Wright who formed our coaching team during the early days in Moldova: advising, supporting, praying for, mentoring and helping me and Helen through so many different situations. Their love, wisdom and support have had a profound impact in my life.

I would like to thank our sending churches and so many faithful prayer and financial supporters, many of whom give sacrificially to support our family. May the Lord bless and repay you for your friendship, encouragement, generosity and partnership in the Gospel.

I thank also all who serve and have served with OM Moldova over the years. It has been, and continues to be a privilege to serve with you.

A big thank you to Peter Lawson, a faithful friend over the years whose comments and editing of this book have been invaluable. Also to my mother for help in editing, but even more so, for putting up with me during those 'teenage years' and whose prayers, encouragement and support have always been such a blessing for our family.

Finally, I thank God for the incredible privilege I have in getting to live this life. Experiencing His transforming power in my life has taught me that our stories, our lives, do not have to be lived and conclude with a question mark!

CHAPTER ONE

Beginning with Adam

This is a story of travel and love, crocodiles and soldiers, life and death, ships and illness, blessing and provision, ugly angels and the KGB, Dracula's castle and hoopoes, holy kisses and miracles, answered prayers and a girl and a voice and a call. This is my story, and, as with so many stories, my story must begin in the beginning – with Adam.

Every Sunday morning my older brother Adam and I would get scrubbed up and climb into the back of the family car and endure the weekly tradition of 'church'. It wasn't that I particularly disliked church, but the old traditional hymns that we sang and the boring, monotonous preaching that we sat through just seemed so irrelevant. What was the point of it all?

As we drove to church I would duck down in the back of the car fearing that one of my friends may see me and realise where we were going. I was embarrassed to admit to my friends that I attended church every Sunday and I was embarrassed to have the same friends around for tea because at our house we would 'give thanks' before every evening meal. I did not want to be known as a religious person and I concluded that church was boring, people who went to church were *very* boring and the whole 'Christian thing' probably wasn't for me. After all, I wanted to have fun; I certainly did not want to live a boring life!

My parents expected me to go to church; it was after all what our family did and had always done on a Sunday morning. When your father is a strict disciplinarian, head teacher of a large local school you learn very quickly to do what you are told. So I endured the weekly outing knowing that the experience would not last long and we would soon be home enjoying a delicious Sunday roast before I could get on with my life, do what I wanted to do and go out and play football.

It wasn't that I didn't believe in God. I kind of accepted that what I heard in Sunday school about God, Jesus and the Bible was true. It made sense to me that we had been created by an all-powerful Creator; I never really could believe that everything had just appeared by chance. So for me, believing in God was not the problem, my issue was that all the religion and 'church stuff' just did not seem relevant for me and what I wanted to do with my life.

———————

Born on the 17th March 1972 in Chichester, West Sussex I spent my first years living with my family on the south coast of England. One of my earliest memories of that time was when I was just two years old. Collecting my older brother from nursery school, my mother and I were met by a concerned teacher who informed the gathered crowd that the school's pet rabbit had escaped. Undaunted by the task I decided that I would find the rabbit and so marching away from my mother I searched under shrubs until there it was … I spotted the bunny munching on some grass near his cage. It is hard to describe the feeling of pride that comes to a two year old when he finds his older brother's nursery's lost rabbit! I had found the rabbit against all odds. I was a hero, and I liked the feeling!

My fame and hero status amongst Chichester's Nursery schools was short-lived as soon we moved along the coast to Worthing, to be closer to Tarring High School where my father was deputy headmaster. Adam and I were both pupils at The Vale First and Middle School where Mum worked as a teacher. Memories of my time at The Vale School include conker competitions, running the gauntlet of 'ice space invaders' where those of us from the younger classes had to dodge lumps of ice thrown by the big kids, the (politically incorrect) 'slave trade' where the younger children were herded up and traded by the older ones and of course kiss chase. I was a fast runner, the girls couldn't catch me – although I did find that it was sometimes fun to let them!

One spring day in 1981 I stood with a small group of children and watched through the window of the staff room the safe return to earth of the first space shuttle; an impressive event for a young boy who had just turned nine and longed for adventure. I daydreamed about being an astronaut, accomplishing something extraordinary, doing something that would be exciting and actually making a difference with my life. I loved sports and spent as much free time as possible playing football with Adam. We would re-enact the great goals and players of the time with me diving around like Peter Shilton and scoring diving headers like Trevor Francis (my Nottingham Forest heroes) whilst Adam would try (in vain) to re-enact the rather more limited glory days of the not so mighty Brighton and Hove Albion.

At the age of eight I was in the upper infant school and had to wait after school for my brother to finish football practice with the Middle School team. As I sat on the edge of the sports field I opened my lunch box and started eating my rather sweaty cheese sandwiches left over from lunch time. The head teacher and football manager Mr McCaffie called to me and asked if I wanted to join in with the bigger boys. I entered the fray energetically and running with the ball from right back scored a goal – my first ever (which was not just in the garden against Adam or Dad). By the end of the training session Mr McCaffie had talked to Mum and I was drafted in to play for the middle school in their next match, away from home at a local rival school. I will always remember the excitement and nerves before the big game. I could not concentrate on school for the whole week leading up to the match as I dreamed about playing – and of course scoring! That feeling of butterflies in the stomach, when excitement battles nerves and confuses me into not knowing if I am nervous or excited or somehow both at the same time is a feeling that I have experienced many times since. The excitement and also pressure that I feel before public speaking today is so similar to the feeling I felt at eight years of age before my first football match.

I wish I could write about how I scored a hat trick on my debut and how I was carried shoulder high from the pitch to the adulation of the older Middle School boys. I would love to write and describe how we fought for the pride of Vale Middle School, but I remember very little about the match apart from the winning (or rather losing) goal. Nowadays the five, three, two formation (with five attackers and two defenders) is rarely used and whilst someone probably should have questioned Mr McCaffie's wisdom in telling our only two defenders to 'stay wide', at the time I was just the young infant school debutee and so I obeyed his instructions and the match was evenly poised at about 8-8 as we entered the last few minutes of the biggest match of my footballing career.

We conceded the all decisive losing goal from a penalty and it was all the fault of the infant school right back. I still remember trying (and failing) to hold back my tears as the referee jogged past me back to centre circle encouraging me to 'keep your chin up son'. The bottom line was that it was me – we had lost because of me. Vale Middle School had lost because the youngest player from the infant school had given away the penalty. I still maintain that it was not really my fault! I was on the near post as the ball flew into the box, there was a scramble and the ball came speeding towards me at waist height. What do you do? What do you do when you are eight years old and you have spent every free moment playing football in the garden with your older brother? When your hero is the great goalkeeper Peter Shilton and you have practised for hours diving around in goal – what was I supposed to do? I caught the ball! It was a good, no, it was a great save! I was on the line and the big heavy ball was moving fast. I didn't punch it away I caught it cleanly, perfect, an amazing save … except I was not the goal keeper. And then I froze, ball in hands! Everyone froze and looked at me … what could I do? Thinking quickly I bent down and stuck the ball between my knees and prayed that no one had seen what I had done. Time stood still. Everyone had seen the most blatant hand ball in the history of football. The only eight year old was standing on the goal line with a heavy brown ball stuck between his legs whilst twenty one nine year-olds, a referee and a scattering of parents all stared – at me! The expression of 'wanting the ground to open and swallow me up' was invented for such a time as that. The opposing team shouted in unison, 'hand ball!' My teammates were horrified and everyone looked to the referee whilst the ball remained firmly lodged between my knees. The referee rather dramatically blew his whistle and pointed to the spot and that was it. The penalty was converted and Vale Middle School lost the match by one goal! Tears, criticism, accusations from the older boys and surely the end of my footballing career.

It would have been very easy never to play again. It would have been easy to give up and return to the infant school where none of the big boys would be present to laugh and accuse me of costing them the game. I cared deeply about what the older boys said about me, their criticism hurt but I realised that I could do it! I could play football. I would show them; I was determined; I would keep playing and would not give up. I also decided that I would never, ever catch the ball on my own goal line again!

So it was that I spent my childhood; playing football, building camps, climbing trees, racing bikes, taking risks, dreaming of adventure and of course, enduring church every Sunday.

Our family had a faith in a God who we heard about and sang songs about for an hour every week but that was just about it, that was Christianity for me. I understood that being a 'church go-er' meant that there were lots of things that you should not do and I felt I needed to be different at school. I knew that I should not use the language that my friends used, that I should try to be 'religious' – whatever that meant – and be a good Christian. For me, being a Christian involved getting bored for an hour each week in church and aiming at some sort of compromise for the rest of the time. I decided to try to be good enough to meet the expectations of my parents, and a distant and strict God, but, at the same time, not be *so* good that I firstly couldn't have any fun and secondly wouldn't give too much ammunition to my friends who would give me a hard time because I was 'religious'.

So it was that as I entered my teenage years I kept my belief in God, my 'Christian faith', as secret as possible. Of course, it wasn't really *my* faith at all. I was following the faith, the religious traditions of my parents. They were good people; they were religious, upright people. I loved and deeply respected them and I wanted to grow up to be like them. I saw how their beliefs affected the way they lived their lives and I was thankful for them and the way they raised me and cared for me. I was even grateful for the way they disciplined me (most of the time) as they clearly wanted me to live a good, righteous life, get a good education and follow in their footsteps. But their faith was … well it was *their* faith, not mine; I believed but could not really see how this belief in God could help me in my life.

Whilst I believed the things that I heard in church, I did have a problem with some of Jesus' words. In one of the rare(ish) moments when I was actually concentrating during a sermon and not day dreaming, I heard that Jesus had said "I have come that they may have abundant life" (John 10:10). When I heard this I thought "no way!" I looked at the carefree lifestyle of so many of my teenage friends. They did not seem to care about what language they used or the dirty jokes they told. They were starting to enjoy life, attending parties, drinking alcohol, having fun staying up late and enjoying life whilst I was trying to be good so as to please my parents and please a God who, if He did exist, seemed to be quite a spoil sport. I was also trying to enjoy life, but always felt that I had slightly less fun than many of my friends because of the constraints of my religion and church attendance. It was my non-church going friends who seemed to be beginning to experience more of the 'abundant life' whilst I was trying my best to live what I thought was a good life. I was willing to believe everything in the Bible. I could believe all the words that Jesus spoke, but claiming that the *abundant life* was found only by his followers … well I looked around at the church go-ers that I knew and whilst they seemed to be living 'good' lives, I did not see much 'life in abundance' being experienced.

It was one Sunday in December when I was around thirteen when it really hit me. I knew my friends could have a lie-in, then take it easy, watch TV, have fun, ride their bikes and play football. But on that particular Sunday I found myself standing at the front of our church dressed in my Mum's old nightie with a tea towel on my head 'acting' as an inn keeper and telling Mary and Joseph that there was 'no room in the inn'. Jesus may know a lot of stuff but he had definitely got this one wrong. 'Abundant life' was not found in my or any church!

———————

In 1982 my father was appointed Headteacher at The Arnewood School in New Milton, Hampshire and so, as a family, we moved west along the south coast to Highcliffe-on-Sea on the edge of the New Forest.

As I hit my mid-teens, earlier dreams of becoming an astronaut or footballer had been cut from my list of realistic future jobs and so I imagined myself with some sort of job that would earn me enough money to have a nice house and a couple of cars. I would also have a beautiful wife, two or three children, a cat, maybe a dog and enough money to take family holidays and live a comfortable life. I didn't know exactly what I wanted to do or be but if a dream existed then that was it. I would be a 'normal' person who would attend church regularly and do good things whilst living in a good house and holding down a good job and raising a good family. Life for me was going to be … good!

Yes, I would be good and go to church but I needed to avoid the extremes – after all people who were 'really radical' Christians were seriously uncool. Most didn't have many friends and looked funny, wore glasses and were picked on, laughed at and rejected by the cool kids. I wanted to have lots of friends and be accepted and so I decided to keep my (parents') faith as secret as possible and hope that no one really noticed that I had beliefs and was different from others. I decided to avoid 'real' Christians – they just were not good for my image.

I probably should have avoided my brother more!

CHAPTER TWO
Still Haven't Found What I'm looking For

Something happened to Adam at the age of fourteen. He started to change and get all 'extreme' in his beliefs about God. He didn't seem to mind going to the school Christian Union where all the kids who didn't fit in with everyone else would meet up each week. He didn't seem to mind giving out silly looking Christian tracts to others, and he would have long discussions with his friends about Christianity. How uncool was that? I always gave the Christian Union meetings on Tuesday lunch times a wide berth. Who would want to be seen attending those sort of meetings?! Adam didn't seem to mind. After one 'mission meeting' at school, he came into my bedroom that evening armed with some funky cartoon tracts, with pictures of a man trying to enjoy life and then being sent to hell because he had not 'accepted Jesus into his life'. Adam told me that he had repented from his sins and now was saved and would go to heaven and that I also needed to repent if I wanted to go to heaven. His sincerity was admirable and did speak to me, but I felt he was being just a little bit extreme. I told him that I was good (there's that word again) and that I did not need to repent because I had never done anything really bad in my life. My teachers thought I was a good boy, my parents thought I was a good boy (most of the time), my friends thought I was a good boy, I thought I was a good boy and God certainly must have thought I was a good boy – after all he had seen the inn keeper drama, the nightie and the tea towel and my embarrassment in front of the whole church – I had suffered for the Gospel! God saw my sacrifice every Sunday morning. He was surely pretty impressed by me and my family.

"Come on Adam – we don't need to be extreme, only really bad people need to 'repent' so as to escape the flames of hell so vividly portrayed in those silly cartoon tracts!"

When I was sixteen I started sixth-form college in Brockenhurst, Hampshire and the word aimless could probably best describe my life and ambitions during those years. I did okay with my studies but like most other young guys my age I just wanted to live life, have some fun and enjoy myself. On Saturdays I travelled around the country with Adam and friends, watching our local team Bournemouth or my childhood team Nottingham Forest play football. Sundays was church (of course) and then playing football for the youth team Highcliffe Hawks in the afternoons. (I had by this stage put behind me the trauma of my first match and was now a constant pick in the centre of midfield for my college and the Hawks' teams). Life revolved around football, music, studying and keeping my eyes open for girls. Church attendance was a necessary part of my week which I tolerated as I felt that 'it was probably good for me'.

I felt somehow that I was different from my friends. I was after all 'religious', a 'church go-er' and something of the 'truths' being presented in all those Sunday mornings seemed to be rubbing off on me and affecting how I was living my life. Maybe I had just been brainwashed into submission. Maybe after constant exposure to church life I had come to accept blindly what had been fed to me in my formative years. But, as I considered the alternatives I realised that I wasn't just blindly accepting. As I thought about it, I was convinced that God really did exist, there were few doubts in my mind about that. I struggled more with the question of 'so what?' So what if God created the heavens and the earth, so what if 'He sent His Son to die on a cross for our sins' … I believed all of that stuff but what relevance did it have for me, a young man attending sixth-form college, studying Mathematics, Chemistry and Physics, watching and playing football in my free time and increasingly interested in girls?

During my sixth-form years I earned pocket money by running a fairly profitable football programme business. I found that by buying thousands of programmes in bulk, and then selling them on to collectors, I could turn quite a profit which financed my footballing travels. I also started listening to, and buying music albums, and the Irish rock group U2 were my favourites. I especially liked the song 'I Still Haven't Found What I'm Looking For' from the 1987 album Joshua Tree as it provoked something within me every time I listened to it. Something in that song resonated with me as it seemed to reflect a truth that I was experiencing in those tumultuous years of teenage emotions. I was a church go-er, I thought myself to be a pretty good person, yet something was missing from my life. I still hadn't found what I was looking for. The problem was I didn't know what it was that was missing, or indeed, if I was supposed to be searching for anything. Maybe I should just concentrate on enjoying myself and not take things so seriously or worry too much. Yet I knew something was missing. Football was great, I loved watching and playing, but still it did not fulfil me on a deeper and more profound level. I didn't really feel that I would find that 'je ne sais quoi' at church either. It just did not seem to be scratching where I was itching – yet I didn't know exactly where I was itching! Maybe getting a girlfriend would be the answer. Maybe I was yearning for 'relationship' whatever that meant – yep, I was sure that was it, I needed a girlfriend.

Adam was at the same college in the year above and continued to be actively involved in the Christian Union along with a small group of people who did not seem to fit in with the rest of us who were trying to be cool and accepted. I attended the occasional Christian event with Adam but still felt that the sort of people who were a part of these meetings were not 'my sort of people'. I was now at an age where I increasingly knew that I had to choose. How was I going to live my life? Would I keep attending church as was our tradition, give it up altogether, or become a radical Bible basher like my brother? The last option really was not worth considering, so I plumped for the lesser of the three evils and decided to continue to attend church but not really get too involved and certainly never wear a nightie and tea towel in a church drama again.

Sometimes I would go to Sunday evening services with Adam and his wacky friends where the music would be a bit livelier and the whole service less formal. I found myself somehow attracted to this newer style of 'doing church'. I had become so used to boring hymns sandwiched between someone praying or speaking in the mornings yet it was different in the evenings, more spontaneous and somehow more real and relevant. One evening service the congregation sang a 'new' song 'Majesty, worship His Majesty'[1]. For the first time in my life I found myself singing a Christian song and kind of understanding what I was singing. As I sang it was as if I was really meaning what I was singing, as if I was singing not just as a form of religion but actually singing to God and acknowledging His Majesty and Sovereignty over everything – even over my life. I felt a sort of connection with God in a way

1 Jack W. Hayford, 1978

24

that I had never before experienced and it was as if something deep within me was awakened at that moment. I didn't tell anyone at the time, I didn't want to show emotion or look somehow 'uncool' but I knew something had happened deep within me. It was as if my theoretical knowledge of God had moved slightly from my head towards my heart and I sensed somehow God's presence in a way that I had not previously known.

It was a sobering moment for me as I realised that I had taken a step along a path that I wasn't sure I wanted to take and from which I sensed that there was perhaps no turning back. I realised that I no longer just believed in the religion of my parents, but that this Christian faith which had always been so distant and 'for other people' seemed to be becoming something that was real also for me personally. In the occasional times when I did stop and think about spiritual matters I felt as if God Himself was smiling down on me and whispering "Matthew, I am real, I want you to really know me and live closely with me. I want to bring the reality of what you have learnt about me from your head into your heart." He wasn't actually speaking in an audible voice, yet there were times when I just knew that He was present; that He wanted to communicate to me. The strange thing was I felt accepted, I felt that God, the all-powerful Creator of the universe actually liked me. It wasn't just me singing some words in Sunday school that 'Jesus loves me'. Rather, it was the dawning of a realisation of an incredible truth – God does actually love me, and He wants to reveal Himself to me!

How do you, how should you react when you realise that you are loved and accepted unconditionally? When you realise that there is Someone higher and infinitely bigger and more powerful than you, who truly cares for and is interested in how you live your life? My problem was that I wanted to be cool and accepted, I wanted to live life to the full and was still distinctly unconvinced that the 'abundant life' was to be found in the church.

I was concerned that I may become like Adam and like all those other boring, un-cool Christians that filled church youth groups. This was the last thing I wanted … and so the year I turned eighteen and was accepted into the University of London I left home and began my journey to freedom.

In September 1990 the freedom began. I left home for the first time and set off for university knowing that life could now really begin. My parents were not going to be there to get me up on a Sunday and take me to church. No one knew about my religious beliefs and secret Christian faith; I could start to live however I wanted to and not feel guilty about it.

The problem was I had chosen to study Mathematics at Royal Holloway College, University of London, which just happened to be the same college where Adam was also studying Maths. What was wrong with me? I would never truly be free if Adam was always around! It was as if someone was directing my steps and keeping me closely linked with Christians even when I had little interest in actually, actively pursuing my faith. After all, you can really start to live at University. You can do stuff that your parents will never find out about, you can live exactly as you like. Now was the time to start experiencing the 'abundant life' that Jesus had mistakenly identified with life in the church. I was eighteen years old and ready to begin living!

For the first year I steered clear of the College Christian Fellowship. The New College Christian Fellowship (NCCF) was led by the sort of people who I had grown used to recognising (and avoiding) over the years. They all seemed to have guitars and U2 LPs and would go around giving each other 'Christian hugs'. They tried to be cool but in my view failed miserably. Adam had become very active in this group of strange, 'out of touch' people but I was far more interested in playing football and hanging out with 'normal' than attending Christian Youth meetings.

My trial for the college football team had gone well despite only getting to bed in the early hours of the morning the day of the trial.[2] I won a place in the second XI playing alongside Adam, but after a couple of matches I was promoted to the first team and a hat trick on my debut sealed my place in the first XI for the next three years. So it was that my student life consisted of football training and matches four or five times a week, sitting through boring Mathematics lectures and hanging out with friends and listening to bands at the University Student Union building. No time for pursuing my hazy Christian faith. At times Adam would try to get me to go to the Christian meetings and I did reluctantly attend a small 'fellowship group' for most of the year but I only occasionally accompanied Adam and a group of students to the local church. Being a Christian was decidedly uncool and not something I really intended to 'be' in public.

As my first year ended I returned home for the summer and tried to keep fit for the start of the new football season and prepare myself for life as a second year student. Adam shocked me that summer with the news that he was going to go on a 'mission trip' to Uganda to help people and tell them about God. I had observed (from a distance) Adam's increasing radical involvement in all things Christian over the last year at college. His greater involvement in the Christian fellowship possibly cost him a place in the first XI football team as he was not so often at football training. It was a matter of significant pride for me that I was in the first XI whilst my big brother only played for the second XI. I did however keep well clear of him when we played 'friendly'

2 For some strange reason a Bournemouth away match against Southend United had attracted me and having missed the last train out of London I had walked for miles only to arrive back at college in the early morning exhausted.

matches for what Adam lacked in skill and finesse he more than made up for with elbows and studs!

To my surprise my parents seemed quite happy and supportive for Adam to be a 'missionary', go off to Africa, do good, wear a pith helmet, grow a beard, contract malaria and get eaten my cannibals. On his return he seemed even more committed to his faith and as he shared about his experiences my mother asked me; "Matthew don't you think it would be good for you to do something like this as well?" I mean "Hello!?" Was she actually serious? My reply was very clear; "Mum, there is no way I am ever going to do something like that!"

I had other plans for my life. I was in control of my life and I certainly wasn't going to go off to some far away country and do who knows what. I was going to finish university; get a good job, get married, start a family and settle down. I would continue on with my Christian religion and maybe even get involved in a local church because I knew it was the right and proper thing to do, but 'going public' with my faith? Missionary, me? No, no and no!

I had no idea that my life was about to change forever.

CHAPTER THREE

How to Impress a Girl

I had spent my first year at university playing football, keeping an eye open for girls and in my spare time, studying, but now I was entering my second year things were about to change. One good thing about being a second year student is that you can pretend to all the first year students that you know your way around the college, are experienced and super mature and it is a great opportunity to meet new people. And so it was that in September 1991 I found myself in the student Union building listening to a visiting band and hanging out with my friends. One first year student, Cath, who had just joined the fellowship group that I fairly regularly attended, happened to be at the same concert, and introduced me to her next door neighbour, a very interesting and attractive girl called Helen Bartholomew.

Helen was really small. Her black hair had been tinted red and she was wearing a purple and green tie-dye top, skinny jeans and big, green, Doc Martin boots. She was so bubbly, energetic and friendly that I immediately liked her – in fact I immediately liked her a lot! I don't really know what love at first sight is – however, I did know from the moment that I met Helen that I wanted to get to know her more. I found her fascinating and over the next weeks sought every opportunity possible to meet up with her. She was studying Classical Studies, and I planned my weekly schedule carefully so as to 'accidently' find myself hanging around outside her lecture venues just as she finished lectures so that I would be able to walk and talk with her between lectures. I found out early on that Helen was a Christian and was getting very involved in the Christian fellowship meetings, so I felt it time for me also to attend and show her what a good Christian I was.

Over the following weeks I went to more Christian youth events than I had attended in the whole of my first year. The fact that Helen was so involved in all of these events was, (I told myself), purely incidental. There were the Thursday evening Christian meetings, the Sunday Church services, the Tuesday evening fellowship groups, the occasional Christian concert on a Saturday evening and even an early Morning Prayer meeting on Saturdays that Helen led. I found myself being totally immersed and surrounded by the sort of people that I had spent my whole life trying not to be associated with. I was even going to the prayer meetings on Saturday mornings – I really had a problem!

I had spent my whole life being embarrassed by my faith and church attendance. I had always tried to hide this aspect of my life from people and now, here I was spending almost every non-footballing/studying moment in the company of Helen and these other 'Christians'. Helen spoke so naturally about her relationship with God, it was clearly the central aspect of her life, and I couldn't help but compare my own understanding of faith and what it means to be a Christian, to her's.

My Christian faith was an 'add on'. It was a belief that I held, but my life was compartmentalised into different parts. I figured that my faith should, and indeed could, be separate from my football, studies and friends – and it certainly wasn't really central to who I was. I did not really like discussing my beliefs because I was somewhat embarrassed and afraid of what my friends would think. I liked to keep my faith private and secret. Helen, on the other hand, spoke openly about her faith and her beliefs really seemed to be at the heart of who she was and all that she did. I was attracted to her, but I was also very much attracted to her Christian faith and the faith of the young people she hung out with. There was a reality, a personal experience of God that to me seemed at times exaggerated, but was without doubt something that I had never really known. It was as if I had been following a religion, trying to get to God, whilst Helen and these other Christians were enjoying a living relationship with a God who was real, present and active in their lives.

One day Helen showed me her Bible reading plan, which included long lists of Bible chapters that she ticked off as she read them each day. I had always owned a Bible and had even brought to University with me a big black one that my parents had given me. It spent most of the time on a shelf above my bed collecting dust. There had been times when I had taken it from the shelf and read small parts of it, but as with my religion and faith in God it so often seemed hard to understand, disconnected and irrelevant to a football playing maths student trying to enjoy life and have fun.

Helen was clearly interested in me – a member of the football team yet also involved in the Christian fellowship – but she also seemed to sense that I was not quite as committed in my faith as she was. I realised that there was no way that she was going to want to be my girlfriend unless I took radical action. So in order to impress her I got a copy of her Bible reading plan and began reading from the book of Genesis. I would show her just what a good Christian I was!

The first weeks were kind of interesting. As I began in Genesis and Exodus to read systematically for the first time, the different Bible stories I had grown up hearing began to come alive and make sense to me. I did begin to struggle as I hit all the laws and rules in Leviticus – but amused myself, and attempted to impress Helen with my new and extensive knowledge of the strange rules and cleansing rites of people who had different coloured spots on their bodies!

My reading of the Bible continued every day for the next three hundred and sixty five days and it would not be an exaggeration to say that my life was completely transformed during that year.

I had, until that time, always compared myself with other people. I thought of myself as a pretty good person – someone who did not really need to repent for my sins because I had never really done anything wrong! For the first time, however, I began to realise that all was not perfect in my life. As I read the Bible, I began to understand more about God and His interaction with humankind. However, I also began to understand more about myself. It was as if God were holding a mirror up in front of my life and I began viewing my life from a totally new perspective. I realised that I was no longer comparing myself with others; that didn't seem so important any more. After all I could always find someone who I thought I was better than. Rather, for the first time, I felt I was somehow glimpsing my life through God's eyes, seeing myself in the light of His Son, Jesus Christ. I was disturbed by what I saw. I realised that there were attitudes in my heart, thoughts in my mind and plans for my future, that were not necessarily honouring to the God who had created me, loved me and who, I began to understand, also had a plan for my life. I had never before realised that perhaps I was not such a good person all the time. Perhaps compared with some of my friends I could consider myself 'good' – whatever that meant – but I had a new frame of reference for my life now and I started to realise that there were things in my life that really needed to change if I was to truly call myself a Christian. I sensed that God did not want me to try to change these things on my own. Instead, it was as if he was offering to do the work and saying – "You cannot do it on your own, but I can, I love you, I know what is best for you, I want to transform your life, I want to make you into the person you were created to be." During that year it was as if my eyes were being opened and I began to understand that God had a plan for me: He wanted me to live in a real relationship with Him rather than just playing at being religious and attending church.

From the autumn of 1991 to the summer of 1992 I found that the more I read the Bible the more I seemed to grow in my understanding of God, His love and His desire to have me live in a close relationship with Him. I also discovered that my thoughts, plans, attitudes and priorities were gradually being changed as I spent more time reading and considering God's Word. It was not that I was becoming more religious, rather it was as if the closer I got to God, the less religious I became, but the more aware I was of the possibility of enjoying an actual relationship with God as I would with a close friend. I felt as if He actually delighted in revealing more of Himself to me. I use the word delight deliberately, for it really seemed that God, the all-powerful Creator of the universe accepted me and yes – even delighted in me. I found that this truth was transforming me and my perspective on life. I still had lots of questions about the Christian faith; in fact I had more and more questions the more I read and studied. Yet it just seemed all right. I realised that I do not have to understand everything and have an answer for every difficult question. Faith was about believing and trusting in One whom I could not prove or see, yet who I knew was there, as real as anything in my life and who really seemed to want to be known.

Not only was I growing in my relationship with God, but I was also getting to know Helen better. I was now attending all the Christian youth meetings and regularly going to church; not because of my parents, not even because Helen was there, (although that continued to be a great motivating factor), but because I actually enjoyed going! For the first time in my life I was enjoying Christian gatherings. To hear speakers talking about the Bible and sharing their faith and experiences with God was fascinating, motivating and challenging. I found that during the worship times at church I could concentrate and really feel that I was drawing close to God. It was as if all that I had learnt about Him over the years, the theoretical knowledge that I had in my head about God and His love, was being realised in my life. My religion was being transformed into a relationship and for the first time I began to understand Jesus' words in John 10:10. The true life, the abundant life could actually be found only when I knew and lived closely with Him. When I accepted His life into my life, only then could I really experience fulfilment and deep peace, joy and happiness. It was as if I had taken the first steps in finding what I had been looking for.

In the spring of 1992 I spoke to the leaders of Ascot Baptist Church, (the church I was attending as a student), and asked if I could be baptised. I had come to understand that baptism was an important step in a Christian's life. I was experiencing change in my life, in my thoughts and attitudes as well as my actions and for me baptism was an opportunity to make public my faith, to acknowledge before God, my friends and myself that I was a Christian, that I was truly committed to following Jesus and that I was not ashamed of the Gospel.

My relationship with God was becoming the most important part of my life but, I still had a problem! As I spent more time with Helen I was increasingly attracted to this lively and committed Christian, but she seemed a little wary of me. She was the same age as me but was a year below me at the University because she had taken a 'gap year' after sixth-form college and served as a 'missionary' in Ireland, working with young people. She often talked about her time "on the mission field" and spoke so clearly about her calling to serve God in missions after she graduated. She was so determined and clear in her calling that – whilst I was attracted to her – I seriously questioned whether she was 'the one for me'. After all, I had very different plans for my life after college which certainly did not include anything to do with missionary work!

My problem was that I wanted to spend more time with Helen. I was growing in my relationship with God and really wanted to impress her. So I decided to do something in the summer of 1992 that would help her see me in a different light. It was the spring of 1992 when a rather extreme and wacky guy from some strange sounding missionary organisation was speaking at our college Christian fellowship. As I listened to him I did not think he was a particularly impressive speaker and I could not follow everything he said. He did however seem pretty excited about his message, telling stories of what God was doing around the world and how Christians were called to get involved in bringing the Gospel/Good News to other people. As he came to the end of his talk and handed out some literature, an idea came to me. "If I go on a mission trip then Helen will be so impressed that she will surely want to be my girlfriend!" Missionary, me? No, not really a missionary as such, but I could just go for a couple of weeks and you know, do some good stuff!

Genius! And what better motivation for going on a mission trip than to try to impress a girl?

CHAPTER FOUR

A Serious Mistake!?

It wasn't until I was sitting on the bus that I realised I had made a huge mistake!

My Dad had dropped me in London and I had registered and boarded one of six buses that were heading to something called 'Love Europe '92', a conference in Offenburg, Germany run by a mission organisation called Operation Mobilisation (OM). I had managed to save some money from my football programme sales and my parents also gave some money and so I found myself on a bus, in the midst of a group of 'super-spiritual Christians' who kept on saying things like "hallelujah!" "Praise the Lord", "let's pray", "let's sing the latest Graham Kendrick classic" – it was a nightmare! As Shine Jesus Shine was sung for the five-hundredth time and the young guy sitting next to me insisted on telling me his testimony sharing about all the miracles he had experienced and the way he saw God working in his life *every single day* – I shrunk down in my seat, closed my eyes and repented to God for my stupidity. Missionary, me? What had I been thinking?

I had signed up for this three week mission trip to impress Helen. OM was putting on a big conference in Germany from where teams would be sent out to different countries around

Europe. We would all be working with local churches, helping them reach out into their communities. It sounded good – it looked good in the brochure, but sitting on that bus I knew that I had made a mistake.

I think God has a sense of humour and that maybe, just maybe, He was laughing a little bit as I sat on that bus. This may not fit your theology – I mean, does God really laugh? At very least it seems to me that He probably found the sight of me in the midst of all those 'super-spiritual Christians' quite amusing. How else can I explain why the over enthusiastic reserve bus driver decided to choose to sit next to *me* and spend the *whole night* explaining to me from the book of Zephaniah (yes it really exists, I checked!) that we should all be helping the Jews return from exile to Israel and thus speed Jesus' return? I didn't have the heart to say to him; "Look mate, I'm just trying to impress a girl, and I don't really want Jesus to return yet because I want to enjoy my life a bit first – and also you are really weird and I have no idea what you are talking about!"

The journey was bad and things did not get much better at the conference. The food was different, the toilets a challenge, sleeping on the floor of a big warehouse with hundreds of other guys was bearable, the football in the break times with the Egyptians was great, but the people were mostly all really weird. There were six-thousand mostly young people there, hopping around, all good, *perfect* Christians, singing the songs, praying out loud (something I was still struggling with) and acting like the sort of Christians that I had spent my life trying to avoid. I was sure that I was the only normal one in the whole place!

The week consisted of sermons, seminars, discussion groups, worship times and preparation times for the evangelistic outreaches that were to follow. I found myself in a small group with people from South Korea, Germany, America, Egypt and Ireland. It was crazy! I heard of a French speaking group and was tempted to join them thinking that I may find praying out loud in French easier than English. I was perhaps optimistic that my GCSE French would stretch that far, I practised … "Mon Dieu, je m'appelle Mattew, merci pour le … pour le … pour le poulet, ou est Jean Pierre? Il est dans le jardin? Merci, Amen". Nope, my French was not up to it; that was not going to work. I knew I would have to master praying out loud in English otherwise people may recognise that I was not one of them, that I was not such a good Christian. I tried to be like the others and reply to every question with a resounding "Praise the Lord!" I even tried adding Hallelujah to the end of each sentence so as to be as 'Christian' as all the others, but it wasn't me, I just felt stupid and miserable and wanted to go home.

One evening a strange looking, skinny, oldish American guy stood up wearing some funny, world map jacket and started to speak about the world and the need to spread the Good News. I had heard these kind of messages before from these 'missionary types'. These sort of people were extreme and their messages were definitely for *other* people. However, as this man called George Verwer, the founder and International Director of OM[3] spoke, there seemed to be a freshness, a reality in what he said that I had never heard before. He spoke with an incredible, seemingly genuine, urgency and passion that just blew me away and I sat there enthralled by this strange looking man jumping about on the main stage pouring out his heart to us all. It was as if God was speaking to me through him, but I was sceptical, God didn't really 'speak' in that way, that sort of thing only happened to other people, not to *normal* people like me!

At the end of the message we were asked to "close your eyes, bow your heads and respond to the Lord". With "all heads bowed and no one looking around," if we felt that God had been speak-

3 See appendix for a brief history of OM

ing to us then we were encouraged to "stand right there in our place as a sign of us responding to God". I had become quite experienced in these sort of situations. Everyone knows that when the preacher says "with every eye closed and every head bowed" that actually means 'sneak a little look and see what others are doing but try not to catch anyone else's eye'. I mean come on; does anyone really keep their eyes closed at such interesting times when you get to see other people crying and stuff? Of course I had to have a quick peek and see if anyone was standing.

The worst thing in that sort of situation is either to be the only one standing or the only one left sitting. I thought I would let others stand and if more than half were standing then I would too. It's always best not to be in the minority in such situations – you don't want people thinking you are either 'over-spiritual' or 'under-spiritual'. Either of which could be embarrassing and definitely uncool. Balance and image are key at delicate times like this.

By the end of the prayer time pretty much everyone was standing (including me – as I didn't want to be the odd one out) and the worship group launched into a song 'I want to serve the purpose of God'[4].

The words were projected by the overhead projector onto the screen and I started merrily singing along with everyone else but then when we got to the chorus I stopped singing.

"*I want to give my life, for something that will last forever*"

I stopped and just stood there. That was it. That was what I wanted to do! A light went on in my mind – maybe also in my heart – and I realised that this was the answer. This was what I had been looking for. For the first time in my life I kind of realised what was *really* important. Not my studies, not football, not a good job in the future, not even my relationship with

4 'I Want To Serve The Purpose Of God' by Mark Altrogge

Helen: it was God – living *with* Him, living *for* Him – that was the priority. I wasn't just being religious, (in fact I had rarely felt so unreligious), but I somehow knew that God was present and I knew that living closely in relationship with Him was all that really mattered. I knew what I wanted to do. Or rather I realised what I did not want to do. I did not want to waste my life. I did not want to just go through the motions of living for myself and getting all the 'good stuff' and doing all the 'good stuff'. I realised in that moment, at that time that I wanted to do something that would make a difference – I wanted to *live my life for something that would last forever*. I finished the song, holding back the tears (after all what would someone think if they saw me crying). Crying in public was seriously uncool and if someone saw me they might think I was 'one of them' and I wasn't, was I? It was all quite confusing – but I was convinced of one thing – I had met with God, or perhaps it was God who had met with me. Something had happened, I felt somehow more closely connected to the God who, it seemed, wanted to reveal Himself to me, of all people.

At the end of the six days in Germany I had registered to join an evangelistic outreach in Estonia! Very few people had heard of Estonia. The Soviet Union had only broken up a year or so earlier and there were lots of new countries on our maps. I had been attracted to Estonia as an option because it sounded remote and exciting, I was up for an adventure and this would surely impress Helen – so Estonia it was!

It was with a sense of relief and also excitement that I left the conference site together with my team. I was one of the appointed drivers. I enjoyed sharing the driving of an old Ford Transit van as we travelled up through Berlin to northern Germany, and then onto a ferry headed for Sweden. We then drove on through Sweden and took a ferry to Finland, drove through Finland and then took a ferry to Estonia. This missionary life was great! I was travelling and seeing different countries and it was all so interesting and exciting. I didn't mind sleeping on floors of churches or in the back of our transit van. I didn't mind the simple food we ate on our journey. I didn't even mind the prayer times and Bible reading each morning, it was all part of the 'missionary adventure' that I had signed up for.

One of the biggest challenges for me was all the very different people in our team. We had young guys from Germany, Sweden and Finland, as well as girls from England, Canada and the US, and we were led by a Finnish couple. Not only were these people from different countries but they also all seemed to come from different types of churches. I had never spent time with such a diverse group of people and quickly found that the way I talked at home and the jokes I could make with my friends in England were not appreciated in this group. I had to change and adapt in order to be understood.

The mosquitoes were a constant challenge, as were the 'squat and drop' toilets, but it was the poverty that spoke to me the most. Estonia had only broken free from the Soviet Union a year earlier and was struggling economically as a result. Christians had experienced persecution under Soviet rule and I found it sobering to hear the stories of suffering and deportation that so many had experienced just because they had proclaimed faith in Jesus Christ. It all seemed such a far cry from the comforts I had grown up with and the freedom to go to church I had always taken for granted.

We arrived at a small Evangelical church in Parnu in the south of the country and from there were sent out to small villages where we would help with some church plants. Small groups of believers had started to meet together in some of these villages and the foreign missionaries were sent to encourage them in their faith and help them reach out to others. We began each day with Bible devotions and prayer and then would go out through the village with local believers inviting children to a 'kid's club' in the afternoon and adults to a Gospel meeting at the local muusikakulle (Music Hall) in the evening where the Good News would be shared.

I enjoyed the games and sports activities with the kids every afternoon and didn't mind being a part of the sketches that we would do in the evening meetings. I found the singing a little difficult. I had never considered myself to be particularly musical and standing up and singing in front of people was quite frankly embarrassing. I found that if I stood at the back and ducked down behind Ola the Swede then I could kind of hide from view. The problem was that as one of the only native English speakers, the group was relying on me to help take more of a central role in the singing of 'Shine Jesus Shine' which seemed to be just about the only Christian song that was known. So it was that we sang about shining – and I tried to allow God's light to shine out from behind a tall Swede.

An hour or so before one meeting I was feeling quite pleased with myself. We had spent the day playing games with kids, giving out Christian tracts and inviting people to the Gospel meeting that evening. The handful of believers in the village had also been inviting friends and relatives and we were expecting around fifty people to come and listen to the foreigners speak about God. We practised the drama which involved someone getting stuck to a chair (representing sin) and then only finding freedom when praying to God. After we had run through 'Shine Jesus Shine' a few times, just to make sure we all knew the words, the team-leader asked us who was willing to explain the drama to the people. There was silence as we all looked at each other. When he asked me to do it I told him in no uncertain terms that this was impossible. I was willing to be in the drama, drive the van, give out tracts, play games with children and even sing 'Shine Jesus Shine', but I was not – EVER – going to speak in public. I tried, of course, to maintain a spiritual maturity during the conversation adding that I felt called to pray more for the team that evening and suggested that perhaps others should be given the opportunity to take a more central role.

Tuukka, I felt, must have been a particularly unspiritual leader, as he just did not seem to discern God's will or indeed understand what I was saying. After insisting that I 'just preach a little' he was off practising 'Shine Jesus Shine' on his guitar whilst I sat, stunned, thinking dark thoughts about this insensitive team-leader who clearly was not in touch with God. My big, black Bible was on my lap and I was shaking so much that I could hardly hold a pen in my hand as I tried to think and prepare what to say. I was NOT a public speaker! I was NOT a preacher! I was not even a Christian quite like the others were *and* I did not even like singing Shine Jesus Shine very much. This was not what I had signed up for!

I do not remember much about that evening meeting other than my shaking legs and dry mouth. The drama went well and I was stuck to the chair for much longer than usual for I knew what was about to follow. Finally, I was free from the chair and I reached behind me for my Bible which seemed to have become much heavier. I stood there in front of a group of people sitting in silence, all looking expectantly at me! Annamarie, a local Christian girl, stood next to me ready to translate for the 'great English evangelist'. I managed to say a few words about the drama and what it represented and then said something about John 3:16 and how God loves us all. I would like to report that people flocked forward at the end of my 'message' with tears in their eyes as they turned to God in their droves – but the reality was that I finished as quickly as I could and hastily invited the team back to the front as I retreated behind Ola to the familiar tune of a well-known Christian song.

But, I had done it! I had spoken in public about my faith. Over the next couple of weeks I did this more and more. I was the one who spoke about the drama. It was strange but the more I did it the more I felt that I really believed the message I was sharing! There was an increasing urgency in my heart and in my message. Many of these people had never heard this Good News. Many of them had never heard what God has done for us and how much He loves us. Some of them would perhaps never have the opportunity to hear again. We travelled, invited, prayed, shared and of course sang *you know what* for the next couple of weeks and I was very aware that God was not only working through our team but He was also at work in my heart – something was different, I was changing! We prayed with a number of people as they publically acknowledged that they wanted to get to know God better and join the local church.

And so it was that during my time on that mission trip in the summer of 1992 I began to understand more clearly than ever before in my life, that God really loves people and sent His Son to die for everybody and that real life is found only when living in relationship with this loving God. My eyes also seemed to be opened to the reality that not everyone has heard about this Good News and that without Jesus people are lost. But most surprising of all, I began to realise that God could use ordinary people like me to help bring His message of hope to people. I began to realise that perhaps I could live my life in such a way as to make a difference in the lives of others. Perhaps I could do something with my life that could have eternal consequences. Was it possible that I had found what I was looking for?

CHAPTER FIVE

Right at Nuremberg

During the year in which I met Helen, not only did I press on with my daily Bible reading and get more involved in the Christian Fellowship at College, but I continued playing football for Royal Holloway College and was also picked to represent the University of London first XI. This meant I was training or playing football six times a week. We played matches against Oxford, Cambridge, the British Armed forces and professional teams from South London. Our 1992 end-of-season tour of Northern Ireland was cancelled due to fears for safety as the IRA[5] were targeting British nationals, but in Spring 1993 we played in a tournament in York against the top student teams in the country. We beat Scotland and Cambridge but lost to the teams representing Oxford and England. The tournament went well, and I became London's nomination to represent Great Britain at the World Student Games that summer to be played in Canada.

It was the beginning of the summer of 1993. I was graduating from University and did not know what I wanted to do after-

---

5 An Irish republican revolutionary military organisation that was active in the United Kingdom.

wards. Playing football in Canada sounded great, but I was fairly realistic that any chance of a career in football had passed me by. When I failed to make the British Team that summer I was not terribly disappointed, or surprised, as I sensed that it wasn't for me. My reading of the Bible that year had assured me that my life was in God's hands, all I had to do was trust Him and walk with Him.

Trust God from the bottom of your heart;
don't try to figure out everything on your own.
Listen for God's voice in everything you do, everywhere you go;
he's the one who will keep you on track.
Proverbs 3 : 5–6 (The Message)

I completed my Honours Degree in Mathematics but did not see the need to hang around for the graduation ceremony. I had more exciting things planned than dressing up and throwing a silly hat into the air. My friendship with Helen had developed through the year, as had my relationship with God. Helen had heard all about my adventures the previous summer and wanted to experience an OM Love Europe summer campaign for herself, so we applied and in July 1993 set off on our first mission adventure together.

There we were together, sitting on a bus driving south through Europe towards the Love Europe 1993 summer conference. Being the seasoned, mature and experienced Love Europe participant that I was, I had been appointed 'bus-leader' by some wise OM staff member in London. It was all so much better than the previous year, having Helen next to me, helping to count people on and off the bus at each Rastplatz (service station). All was well until we got to the Nuremberg ring road and discovered that the driver did not know the way to the conference site. After some time of driving up and down autobahns we approached another intersection. The bus driver, seemingly to himself, muttered "which way, which way?" I nearly fell off my seat when Helen shouted "Turn right!" The driver swerved precariously and took the right. I looked at Helen in wonder. Wow! God had given her a word of knowledge; we were blessed to be travelling in the presence of a super-spiritual modern day saint! I forget at exactly what stage I started to feel awkward. Maybe it was when I picked up some rather non-Christian mutterings coming from the driver. Maybe it was about halfway through his thirty-seven point turn on the narrow country road, or perhaps when he demanded to know who had confidently, (and wrongly), shouted "turn right" that I began to question why I had agreed to be the bus leader. Helen seemed unfazed, and indignantly told me "well someone had to make a decision!" I said nothing, and shrank down in my seat. What sort of a person was I falling in love with and what was I even doing here anyway?[6]

The conference that year was much more enjoyable for me as I had Helen to meet up with between the seminars and sessions. Again some six thousand Christians from all around the world split off into teams and headed off to work with local churches in every corner of Europe. Whilst Helen went to Sweden on a team, I had chosen to join one of the teams going to Russia for four weeks.

Having slept on the floor of an OM bus from Nuremberg to Prague, I then flew together with a team of young people to Moscow. We were diverted to St Petersburg due to a storm but finally made it to Moscow and took the metro to the train station where we spent the night sleeping on the floor. Sleeping is perhaps an exaggeration. Ivan, one of our team-members, and an Australian,

6 We have driven past Nuremberg dozens of times in the years following this incident and I never can resist shouting "turn right" every time Nuremberg appears on a sign. Helen's sense of direction, map reading skills and ability to communicate clearly and give directions at the right time never cease to contribute to stress free and peaceful family road trips!

(of Russian descent), was convinced that we were going to be robbed and murdered by the mafia as we slept, and so he insisted on staying awake and standing watch all night. I was too tired to care, and managed to rest a little, which was good because we still had a two day train journey on the Trans-Siberian railway ahead of us.

Ufa, in the Ural mountains was our destination. We were to be based in the only Baptist church in the city of a million people and were to help the church in their outreach programmes. As in Estonia, a year earlier, I was struck by the poor standard of living that I saw all around me and again realised how privileged I was to have grown up in a prosperous part of the world. The work we did for those four weeks was fairly similar to that which I had experienced the previous summer in Estonia. Together with local Christians we visited hospitals, kindergartens and market-places, sharing our faith through songs, dramas, testimonies and literature. I sat through countless long church services that would last two or three hours. During those four weeks of church services I managed to read through the whole of the New Testament and I perfected the art of sitting in long boring services, not understanding anything but looking up, smiling and nodding on occasion to give the impression of total engagement with what was happening. This art has not left me and still is employed in many situations today!

It was in Russia that I first recognised the fixation that Soviet peoples seem to have for cabbage. Now I had considered myself a fairly balanced person, liking carrots, potatoes, lettuce, tomatoes, green beans and even broccoli as much as the next man. But cabbage? Cabbage was always on a par with Brussels sprouts in my mind, something to eat if you are served it so as to be polite, but not a food that should really be promoted above other vegetables. I learnt many things during those weeks – not least that in Russia, cabbage takes a central role in everyday life! Cabbage soup, cabbage rolls, cabbage pies and even cabbage sandwiches were served us throughout each day.

The boys on the team were sleeping on the balcony of the church and we always had to be careful to get dressed early enough in the morning before the *babushkas* (old ladies), would turn up for choir practice. After a couple of cabbage-filled weeks my stomach could take no more. The toilet was a hole behind an asbestos screen in the courtyard of the church and I always dreaded my visits there. One Saturday night I lay down on my sleeping-bag feeling particularly unwell and wondered, not for the first time, why I had chosen to spend my summer in a remote city in central Russia.

As the *babushkas* arrived for choir practice, before the main meeting, I realised that I was not going to be able to sit through the service. I had never felt so ill in my life, something – not only cabbage – that I had eaten the day before, clearly didn't want to stay inside me. As I lay on the balcony floor and the church filled up I realised that I needed to pay an urgent visit to the outdoor toilet. The problem was that this would involve getting dressed, clambering down the stairs past the people in the back of the church, through the courtyard, to the toilet, hoping that it was not occupied. I had such pains in my stomach that I seriously doubted that I would be able to move, and my fear was that if I decided to move then things within me would move even faster.

I closed my eyes and prayed as I had never prayed before. There was no answer. Jesus didn't return. Maybe God didn't exist after all. If anything the discomfort in my stomach was worse. The service started and I knew I had no choice, when you have got to go, you have got to go! I managed to get dressed without being seen above the bannister, which was in full view of the pastor and the choir, and I crawled to the stairs. Every movement brought waves of nausea and added great urgency to my quest. I had planned the route in my mind and now I knew there was no turning back.

Struggling down the stairs I frantically pushed my way through the people at the back of the church, some of whom tried to shake my hand and wish me God's peace! The peace of the Lord was far from my mind as I fought past them and managed to arrive at the toilet just in time. To my considerable relief, it was not occupied. Being ill is one thing. Being ill and a long way from home another. Being ill, a long way from home, with a non-flushing outside toilet and the promise of another two weeks of cabbage just takes everything to a whole different level. What was I doing here – surely nothing warranted this sort of suffering?

Over the years I have eaten a variety of foods which have included iguana in Guyana, squid in Greece, stingray in Malaysia, plantains in the Caribbean, 'mild' curry in India, chicken hearts in Brazil, grits in the US, 'animal' kebabs in Azerbaijan, some sort of fishy/sea-weedy thing in South Korea and did I mention cabbage in Russia? I have always found that whilst it is polite, important and fun tasting local foods, there is nothing like familiar foods and to my shame I confess to experiencing great joy at times when I have come across McDonalds, Pizza Hut or KFC in places such as Tbilisi, Bangkok, Cairo, Belgrade, Seoul and Georgetown.

Due to some need to economise, it was decided that whilst we had travelled to Ufa in a second-class carriage, we were to use third-class on the way back to Moscow. It was mid-summer with the temperature well into the thirties Celsius and the windows of the carriage did not open due to the Eastern European's fear of draughts. We found ourselves in an open carriage with some sixty other travellers many of whom were already days into their Tran-Siberian journey to Moscow and had not seen a shower for quite some time. After the first night I braved the toilet and then tried to return to my bed. As I opened the door of the carriage an aroma of stale air, smelly feet, rotten cabbage, (to which our team had certainly contributed), quite literally took my breath away.

How had I possibly slept in there? I found it physically difficult to re-enter the carriage and warned my team-mates not to leave. Sometimes you do not know how good, (or bad), something really is until you have something to compare it with.

After visiting Lenin's waxy-looking body in Red Square and finding to our joy that McDonalds had just opened in Moscow, and that cabbage had not been added to Russian Big Macs, we boarded our plane back to Prague. There was still a drive back to England across Europe ahead, but I was going home after six cabbage filled weeks! As we took off from Moscow I heard a voice. Now I was not, (and probably still am not), the most spiritually-minded person in the world and I do not really hear voices, but on that flight, as we took off I heard a voice. It was not an audible voice but I heard it as clearly as if the person next to me were speaking. As the plane ascended, I looked down on the lights of the huge city spreading out below me, and the Voice said "Matthew do you see this city? Think of all the people living here and in the whole Soviet Union – I am calling you to serve here, I am calling you to serve as a missionary in this part of the world." I sat there stunned and sensing God's presence in a special way. It was a strange experience but I knew without a shadow of doubt that one day I would be back in that part of the world.

Whilst in Russia I kept a diary and towards the end of my time there I recorded something of my experiences in trying to share the Good News with people.

"I know that this is what I want to do, actually I am not sure if I want to, but I know I can do nothing else. I realise that God Himself is calling me to serve Him on the mission field."

There it was, I had written it, I had said it – and Lord have mercy, I felt as if I was turning into a 'proper Christian' – the very sort of radical, extreme, over the top sort of Christian that I had always tried to avoid. I was trying to be a normal person, I didn't want to be extreme, I didn't feel like a missionary and my stomach certainly was not called to be a 'missionary stomach', but I had a sense of being called – what was I letting myself in for?

So, as a recently-graduated, football-loving, young guy who had just sensed God's calling to the former Soviet Union I was struck with the question what should I do next? … Within a few months I would be on a flight to Senegal, preparing to sail across the Atlantic Ocean to the Caribbean!

CHAPTER SIX

Adventures at Sea

Jonah ran away from his calling and took to sea. So it was that in the spring of 1994 I also found myself on a ship in the middle of the Atlantic Ocean. We sailed from Senegal, in Western Africa, for ten days without seeing land and with the sky bigger, darker and more beautiful than I had ever imagined. Then, just off the coast of Cuba, the storm hit, and this time it wasn't cabbage that was my problem.

I wasn't really running away from God. Whilst I was beginning to sense God's calling to the former Soviet Union, I was also attracted to adventure. It would be great to say that I grew up reading the exciting mission stories of David Livingstone, Hudson Taylor and William Carey, but I didn't. Instead it was the Famous Five, Huckleberry Finn, The Hardy Boys and Willard Price's Hal and Roger who helped to form my adventuresome spirit while growing up. The adventures and risks that these fictional characters took certainly impacted my life and so when I heard of a 'Mission Ship' which carried Christians from country to country to share the Gospel, well I was excited to sign up. I had time on my hands. I had graduated and wanted to take a year out to travel and do some exciting things before Helen would graduate and I could maybe consider settling down and getting on with my life as a regular person.

I had spent a couple of months, after my time in Russia, volunteering with the OM Greater Europe team, based in Austria. For years, OM missionaries from that base, had been smuggling Bibles and Christian literature into the former communist countries of Eastern Europe and the Soviet Union where political regimes had not permitted freedom of religion. So, for two months I served with this team doing many practical odd jobs: learning to build walls, pour concrete and pick people up from the airport. I also helped import Christian books into Hungary, Poland and Czech Republic, as well as travelling into the Ukraine to be a part of evangelistic outreach-teams. What a time of growth this was for me as I met people who were serving, and indeed had served for decades, as missionaries in Eastern Europe. These were people who seemed so dedicated and committed to the task of bringing the Gospel to those in Eastern Europe who had never heard. I felt humbled to work with them, was challenged by their commitment to prayer and passion for their ministry, but I was also encouraged that they seemed (mostly) to be pretty normal people! I had already planned my sailing adventure, but felt sure that God was calling me back to work with that team of people serving into Eastern Europe, sometime in the future.

It was early 1994. Helen was finishing her final year at University and I was on the Youth with a Mission (YWAM) Mercy Ship, The Anastasis, as part of a Discipleship Training Programme. The programme consisted of Bible study as well as learning skills to share the Gospel effectively. Three months on the ship studying, as well as taking part in practical chores, were followed by a two month mission outreach. My home church, Ashley Baptist in New Milton, England had agreed to send me on this training programme and they, together with parents and some other Christian friends generously covered my costs.[7]

It was when I was pouring concrete ledges in a bathroom in the prow of the ship that I realised that we were rocking considerably more than usual. The storm was probably not the most violent imaginable, and I was not really running away from God, so did not offer myself to be thrown overboard. The storm was, however, enough to send me to my bunk and the nearest bathroom. I spent a day repenting of everything I could think of and praying for land.

For three months I lived on the ship as part of the international crew. As I followed a disciplined study programme; read my Bible daily and fellowshipped with Christians from all over the world who were also serving on board, I was struck constantly by the question – "What do I want to do with my life?" Again and again the words – "I want to live my life for something that will last forever" came back to me as I sought God about what to do in the future.

Helen and I had been friends for two and a half years and she also was soon to graduate. After my time in Russia and Austria, I had started to think of serving God as a missionary for more than just my gap year, but was unsure how being married fitted into these plans, and anyway, was Helen 'the one', how could I be sure? She had long talked about a calling to serve God as a missionary – should we get married and walk that road together? It was a very helpful time in our relationship being apart for nearly six months. At a time before emails, mobile or smart phones, we spent hours writing to each other, waiting for letters and booking phone calls, and our relationship was enriched hugely as we spent that time apart writing, thinking, praying and dreaming about the future.

---

7 Whilst supportive, my parents were not too excited about having to sign a paper describing what should happen to my body were I to die at sea!

After three months of study, fellowship and work on board the ship I was placed on a team that was going to work with churches in Guyana, South America, for the next two months. I knew very little about Guyana. I had read the terrible story of the Jonestown massacre where some crazy religious guy had forced hundreds of his followers to commit suicide *en masse*. This had happened in 1978, some sixteen years earlier, but people we met still talked about this tragedy and asked questions about it.

As I worked on the mission team for two months, we travelled to a number of regions, trying to encourage Christians in their faith, sharing the Gospel and the hope and new life that we have in Jesus. The conditions were challenging as it was hot and humid all the time, and our clothes were never completely dry. Our mosquito nets kept out some bugs, but giant flying cockroaches would sometimes be found in the morning *inside* our nets and we shared accommodation with rats and huge spiders the size of my hand. I felt like a real missionary, living in humid, jungle conditions and it struck me that I was doing exactly the sort of thing I had assured my mother I would never do just a couple of years earlier. I seemed to have changed so much!

In the village of Laluni we bathed in the creek every morning and spotted crocodiles with the locals at night. One evening we paddled our dugout canoe down the creek, with the water just about lapping over the sides, as our torches picked out pairs of red eyes in the reeds. Neville, an Amerindian friend, (who made a profession of faith whilst we were there), chose a pair of eyes that were not too far apart indicating a smaller crocodile and with some trepidation we paddled closer and closer. We pulled alongside the eyes and just as I was readying my camera, Neville leapt forward almost capsizing the canoe. A machete that I had not previously seen struck the water just behind the eyes and there was a huge splash and thrashing around in the water that nearly overturned our canoe. To my horror Neville dragged the writhing crocodile into the canoe. I tried to put on a brave face but realised how close we had all come to falling into the pitch black water filled with crocodiles. Some of the team refused to wash in the same river after that, but I found it quite exciting to bathe every morning knowing that I was swimming with crocodiles.

Whilst the memory of Neville and the crocodile will always stay with me, there were other experiences during my time in Guyana that impacted my life as much as any other up until that time.

Within days of first arriving in the capital, Georgetown, our team were invited to lead an evening service in a local church. We were to share testimonies, perform a drama and sing, and I was pleased to see that our team knew more songs than just 'Shine Jesus Shine'! After my first stumbling efforts at public speaking in Estonia, I had gained a little more experience in Russia, and had even preached my first sermon in a church in Ukraine a few months earlier. I was far from being an experienced preacher, but I enjoyed the challenge of preparing messages and trying to communicate with people. So I volunteered to give the main message that evening.

I felt that familiar feeling of nerves and excitement in my stomach as my Bible weighed heavily on my lap and I prayed and thought about what to share. I was nervous but began to write down some thoughts based on Jesus' Great Commission to share the Gospel to all peoples. As the evening approached we went through the programme as a team. I was to preach just after Harvard from Norway shared his testimony. I saw that Harvard was sitting on a chair on the terrace, praying, looking even more nervous than I was feeling. So I went over to him and placing a hand on his shoulder, I prayed for him to have courage and be able to communicate clearly what God wanted him to share. As I prayed for him, I felt someone gently place their hand on my shoulder and was encouraged to know that someone was also praying for me and my message. When I finished praying I saw that Harvard was feeling a little better and I too felt an incredible peace and reassurance that God would give me the words to speak that evening; I sensed that I did not need to be afraid, it was going to work out. I was so encouraged and turned to see who had been praying for me and then I realised that there was no one there. The other team-members had left the room earlier. I went out into the hallway but no one had been on the terrace with us. It was the strangest experience. I had felt a hand gently on my shoulder, reassuring and filling me with peace and yet no one was there.

I preached that evening and sensed God's presence in a special way as I challenged the listeners to share the Good News with others. I did not understand how I spoke so clearly and seemingly with authority. I had never experienced the ability to speak in public so boldly before. I lay in bed under my mosquito net that night questioning what I had felt. I knew that a hand had been placed on my shoulder. A hand that comforted, reassured, and in some way confirmed to me that what I was doing was from God. I had asked around and no one from the team had been there or touched me. I had been alone with Harvard, yet I knew that we had not been alone! I was confused. I just felt that this sort of thing did not happen to people like me, but I knew what I had felt and how I had experienced an incredible sense of peace and, well, God's presence! Beyond a shadow of a doubt I knew that God was with me, and I was doing what I was supposed to be doing. That sense of God's presence and approval remained with me during my time in Guyana.

I knew, during those two months of being a 'real' missionary that I was growing as a Christian. I was reading my Bible every day, taking part in kids' programmes, youth events, visiting rural communities and sharing my faith with people. I preached simple sermons in many of the evening Gospel meetings in local churches and saw people respond to the call to commit their lives to follow God. I was growing in my understanding of what it really meant to be a follower of Jesus Christ, and yet I still didn't know what I wanted to do with my life. Was I really being called to be a missionary long term? I wondered if I shouldn't just finish that mission trip, go back to England, be a 'normal' person, get a job, get married and end up trying to be a good Christian back in England. Surely that was enough!? Yet I had a sense that God had placed, and was placing a calling on my life. I was both excited and just a little scared.

One morning it was my turn to lead devotions for the team. I chose a Bible verse and shared some thoughts on it and then put a cassette into the stereo, wanting to play a song that had become special to me in recent months.

I'll obey and serve you
I'll obey because I love you,
I'll obey my life is in your hands
For it's the way to prove my life
When feelings go away
And if it costs me everything
I'll obey[8]

As I pressed play, the sound of the song filled the room and something happened that is difficult to explain. As the music played I started to cry. I didn't just cry but I really cried. In fact, I wept absolutely uncontrollably. Now I had been brought up basically with the understanding that "real men don't cry". Men do not make a fuss, we control our emotions, we don't make a scene and try to keep a good old British stiff upper lip at all times. Well, I was not in control of my emotions that morning. I could not

8 "I'll Obey" By Jim Custer, Tim Hosman © 1983 C.A. Music and sung by Bill Drake, OM Arts International

stop crying, yet I simply did not care what anyone else thought. Psalm 42 verse 7 speaks of "deep calling unto deep" and as I look back on that experience in a morning devotions in a small house in the jungle of Guyana, I realise that this best describes what was happening to me. My spirit, deep within me, was in some way connecting with God in a way that perhaps I had not experienced before. Until that moment I had always known that God had His hand of protection upon me from the beginning of my life. I felt that I had been growing closer to Him for some years, but that morning a deeper transaction took place between me and God.

As I listened to the song, the words became a prayer and I knew that deep within my spirit, I was communicating with God in a more profound way than I ever had before. I was praying the words of the song *"if it costs me everything, I'll obey"*, and as the music played I wept as I had a sense of God simply smiling down on me. A realised deep within my soul that He loved me! He accepted me as I was! He was pleased to call me His son! He even rejoiced in me! It was these truths that melted my heart that morning and reduced me to a blubbering wreck.

I sensed that God was confirming the calling that I had sensed at times over the last year or so. As I wept I knew that the words of that simple song were my response to God. Deep within my spirit, in a place that only God knew about, I was saying; "Yes Lord. I will obey – even if it costs me everything – I will obey!"

It is a scary thing to pray that and really mean it, especially when you acknowledge that you are speaking to the all-powerful, Sovereign God and Creator of the Universe. I knew that I was already a Christian but at that moment something happened as I deeply and sincerely committed myself to follow Him, whatever it would cost. Perhaps I wept because I knew I had, at that moment, died to myself and my life was truly no longer in my own hands. I knew that I no longer lived but Christ lived in me – yet the tears I shed were not tears of sadness but tears of joy.

So it was that after my five month adventure on the ship and then in South America, I flew back to England. So much had happened and I felt I had changed so much, but two important things had been confirmed in my mind. Firstly, I knew for sure that God had called me to serve Him on the mission field. Secondly, I knew that I wanted to marry Helen Bartholomew – but I had come to a point where I was willing to *not* marry her if it was not God's plan.

CHAPTER SEVEN

Where is Moldova Anyway?

It was God's plan!

I am sometimes surprised when I hear someone struggling with – "trying to know God's will for my life". I cannot really recall major difficulties in knowing God's will in the many decisions that I have had to make over the nearly three decades of walking with Him. I have come to understand, that if we love Him with all our heart, seek Him and take time to listen, and learn to recognise His voice; then we can move ahead in life, confident that we are in the centre of His will. God loves us, He knows what is best for us and it is wonderfully liberating to know that He wants to walk hand in hand with us through life.

In their hearts humans plan their course, but the LORD establishes their steps. (Proverbs 16:9)

For me, a lack of peace usually suggests that things are not right and I may be moving in the wrong direction. I have never been one for just sitting around and waiting to see a hand writing on the wall, describing clearly the way ahead. I mean, how often do you get your future mapped out exactly for you? There is a time for fasting, praying, seeking counsel and waiting patiently, but often I have found that as we live with God and bathe our decisions in prayer, we need to press on, move ahead, 'push on doors' and they will either open or that lack of peace and a deep inner conviction will confirm that it probably is not God's will.

It was in the summer of 1994 and I had warned God that I was going to propose to Helen, and that He would need to stop me if this was not His plan. I sensed great peace and assurance that Helen was 'the one' and our relationship was of Him – so I went for it. Having prepared a surprise meal for Helen, I got down on one knee and asked her to marry me. I was quite taken aback when her response was: "Are you serious?!?" I promised her that I would probably never be rich and that I was called to serve on the mission field but she still said "Yes!" She had no idea what she was letting herself in for!

We set a date for November 4th 1995 for our wedding, but knew we would not be together for much of the following sixteen months. Helen had been so encouraged by the stories that I had told her from my time with YWAM, that she also had applied to join a Discipleship Training School (DTS). So whilst I (re) joined the Greater Europe team of Operation Mobilisation in Austria, Helen went to Spain and once more we were to communicate only by letter and the occasional phone call for the next six months. Again, we found our relationship deepened as we wrote to each other and were able to share our concerns and dreams for the future together.

My first visit to Eastern Europe in 1994 was to Romania. Only a few years earlier, Romania had broken free from Ceausescu's communist rule and was struggling to rebuild itself. As I left Austria I was excited. I had heard about this land of mountains, poverty, orphans, mystery and Count Dracula! I had also read about the spiritual-awakening, which had taken place since the fall of communism, with tens of thousands turning to Christ and huge churches springing up all around the country. I was travelling with two ladies, Jana from America and Karin from Sweden, and some days after leaving the base in Austria, we found ourselves in the city of Iasi, in the far east of the country. We delivered books to our distributor there and then set off on the drive down towards the city of Galati, further to the south, where we were to visit the OM Romania team. As we drove along beside a river I looked on the map and saw that we were driving very close to the former Soviet Republic of Moldova. There was something exciting and fascinating about the villages I could see across the river in this mysterious country. When we stopped for lunch I wondered what it would be like to go there. Before we set off again we decided to pray for Moldova – this 'unknown' country that was literally a stone's throw away across the river. I prayed what I considered to be a reasonable prayer of blessing for the country and that God would strengthen believers and his Church there. Then Karin began to pray. She prayed for Moldova generally and then she finished her prayer with *"and Lord please would you send Matthew and Helen there as missionaries one day."* Where had that come from? Surprised, amused, intrigued and somewhat nervous I asked her why she had prayed in this way. She just smiled and shrugged and from that moment I could not get this strange, mysterious new country of Moldova out of my mind.

After two weeks of travelling, we arrived back in Austria and I had two things on my mind. Firstly, I wrote to Helen and said that I felt God may be calling us to serve Him in Moldova. Secondly, I spoke to the OM leaders and asked what OM was doing in Moldova and whether I could take a trip there.

Helen shared my excitement about Moldova – the OM leaders did not.

I can understand why the mission leaders did not seem to share my enthusiasm for beginning a ministry in this new country. Here was a naive twenty-two year old new recruit, who had just joined the team and been given responsibility for literature distribution in Romania, talking about starting some sort of OM ministry in a new country. OM teams in all the other Eastern European countries were understaffed, and so the thought of starting a new work in a new country was probably not so sensible. Anyway – who was this young inexperienced British guy who had only just joined OM?

In the 1970s and 80s OM-ers had visited the Moldovan Republic when it was still part of the Soviet Union and smuggled Christian literature to believers there. Since the declaration of independence in 1991, OM had not been involved in any ministry there, and very little was known about the country other than it was said to be very poor. On all of my visits to Romania for the next months I started asking friends if they knew about Moldova and if they had contacts there. Most Romanians warned me that it was a 'bandit, mafia country' and dangerous to visit, but the more I heard things like that the more I wanted to go.

By the spring of 1995 Helen had completed her DTS and joined me in Austria. She lived in the single-girl's accommodation, but worked together with me in the literature distribution department. We planned trips into Romania together, (always taking along a third person as a chaperone), and spent a lot of time trying to build up a list of contacts in Moldova with a view to visiting.

The OM leaders in Austria were, I think, starting to get tired of my constant pleas to go to Moldova. Every Thursday at the OM prayer night I would urge everyone to pray for Moldova. The more we prayed, the more God seemed to give me a love for the country, and the desire to visit just kept on growing. By June 1995 we had a list of a dozen or so people who lived in Moldova. These were Christians who had at some time visited Romania, or had some sort of contact with someone we knew in Romania, and so they had been added to our list.

We applied to the Moldovan embassy in Vienna for visas. The staff at the embassy were very friendly but rather surprised that someone was wanting to visit their country. I got all my paper-work together and applied for visas and was told that the visas would cost one hundred US dollars each. The staff rather apologetically explained that they did not receive any money from Moldova for their costs and so needed to make money on the sale of visas and 'other business'. I was not sure what 'other business' meant, although I did hear on the news at the time, that the Moldovan Minister of Justice was arrested at the border trying to leave Austria in a stolen car! We did not have the money for the visas but prayed that God would provide. Finally, on our fourth visit to the embassy to have the visas stamped into our passports, we were told by a smiling embassy worker that an exception had been made, and we were to be given the visas free of charge.

And so it was that with much excitement and some trepidation, we added seven days to one of our trips to Romania, and headed for Moldova. We had packed the van full of children's clothes and food, (having heard that there were great humanitarian needs in the country), and collected recently printed Christian tracts and children's picture brochures from Romania as we travelled through. Our chaperone and translator was a young Romanian Christian called Gabby, whom Helen had met on her DTS the year before. Gabby, like many Romanians, had heard and fearfully repeated to us stories of the Moldovan mafia and bandits and poverty that even drove some Moldovans to sell human-flesh in the market-places. So it was with a sense of unease that around mid-day on June 13th 1995 we arrived at the Albita, Romania/Moldova border crossing.

We had terrible problems with the Romanian customs officials as we tried to leave the country. We had insufficient paperwork for the humanitarian aid and literature that we had collected from Romania. We spent hours arguing and persuading them to let us pass. Eventually they let us go saying "anyway the Moldovans will never let you in so you will soon be back". As we crossed the river Prut, between the two countries, it was as if we were entering another world. Young, bored soldiers with guns stopped us and ask for cigarettes or beer before we crossed a bridge and were on Moldovan soil for the first time. Until then we had thought that Romania was poor, but what struck us about the Moldovan border was the sense of dereliction. We drove towards some old, seemingly disused buildings with broken windows surrounded by weeds. There was no one there. No other cars at the border at all. No one at all was entering Moldova and perhaps more worryingly, no one was leaving! As our van pulled up to the first of many check points, we were surrounded by serious looking border border guards, customs officials and soldiers. Mostly they seemed pretty bored and were just happy to have something to do, and the checking of paperwork was a formality once they saw our visas. We told them we were bringing humanitarian aid into the country and they were very friendly and welcoming. We did notice that Gabby our Romanian translator was struggling, and realised for the first time just how much Russian was spoken in Moldova, and that the Moldovan dialect of Romanian was not always easy for Romanian speakers to understand.

The Romanian guards were wrong. We had been warmly welcomed in to this new, wonderful country. We passed many different checkpoints and controls and I was back in the former Soviet Union and in Moldova for the first time. Our joy was short-lived as some five kilometres through the border we were stopped by armed guards and police and sent back to the border. We had to pay for an extra insurance paper before returning to the last check point where we had to go through all the checks again. We then had to pay road taxes, ecology taxes and a number of other 'payments' that we never really understood, and began to believe that perhaps the Romanians had been right.

As we finally drove away from the last check point a policeman stopped us again. He said something in Russian and then seeing that we didn't understand, switched to Romanian. "Where are you going?" Gabby explained we were going to the capital, Chisinau and he started speaking excitedly to Gabby gesturing towards the road ahead. We were warned not to take the 'Poltava' road through the forest as he said that there were bandits along that road. He suggested that we took a longer road through the villages which he said was safer. The look on Gabby's face as he relayed this information to us was a picture. All he had heard about Moldova, all his fears were being confirmed – this journey was becoming more and more interesting.

We took the road through the villages, and drove fifty kilometres or so hardly seeing any other cars. We noticed also that there were so few horse and carts compared with Romania and asked Gabby about this. He looked at us incredulously and said, "Only rich people can afford horses", as if we were stupid – we really were entering another world.

Just past a small town called Hincesti we knew we were getting close to Chisinau and decided to stop for a picnic. I was not actually hungry, but the reality of being in a *very* foreign country was sinking in, and I felt I needed to stop and 'regroup' a little. We pulled off the road into a forested area and as Helen prepared some sandwiches I lay down and closed my eyes. It was then that I heard a voice. It was not an audible voice but it was as clear as if someone was standing next to me whispering in my ear. I heard this voice in a similar way to hearing a voice on the aeroplane leaving Moscow two years earlier – but that was where the similarities ended.

The voice I heard in the forest in Moldova was not a soft, comforting, reassuring voice – it was a harsh, sneering, threatening, 'dark' voice. "What do you think you are doing? Do you really think you can make a difference and accomplish something for your god here?" Where had that come from? Someone, something had spoken to me. The hairs on my arms stood on end and I felt a fear that is difficult to describe. It was difficult to speak or even pray. As I lay there in the Moldovan forest I really wanted to go home. I did not want to be there. Whatever, or whoever that voice was had flooded me with fear. I look back at it now and smile as I remember, but at the time I was not smiling. This had not just been my imagination. I had heard a voice as clear as if someone had been sitting next to me – and I was scared! I did not tell Helen and Gabby what had happened as they both already seemed quite nervous. Instead we gave thanks for the food, prayed for God's protection and direction, ate our sandwiches and drove off towards the capital city.

As we entered Chisinau we were stopped by more policemen who rather bizarrely wore black cowboy hats. We were to learn that after gaining independence from Moscow the police force had voted to wear these hats (based on the design of Canadian Mounties). In those days it was very unusual for us driving a foreign vehicle to travel more than half an hour, without being stopped and having our paperwork checked, by the 'cowboy police'. Apart from old Soviet buses, Mercedes mini-buses and a smattering of old Soviet cars that I had only ever seen in films, we were, as far as I could see, driving the only foreign vehicle on the roads. It was when we finally found ourselves in the centre of Chisinau that I started seriously to question our sanity.

I had a list of names of people from all over the country who were said to be Christians. We had managed to speak by phone to someone from the Pentecostal Union of Evangelical churches and they had sent the invitation letter to the embassy for our visas. We had told them the day we planned to arrive but had not been able to communicate clearly in English by phone our plans, which was quite good really because we ourselves did not really have any plans. We just kept on praying and asking God to lead us, protect us and show us what to do.

Gabby eventually found a public telephone, changed some money, bought a coupon for the phone and called the number.

Within a very short time, two men had arrived in a car, shook hands with us and escorted us through some remote back streets to a house. We were taken into a back room where eight men were standing around a table at which sat an older man. All the men wore suit jackets over shirts which had the top button done up. No one smiled; they all just stood and looked sternly and suspiciously at us as we stood before them.

Now we had been travelling at that stage for five days from Austria, through Hungary, having spent some time in Romania before coming to Moldova. We had not washed or showered during that time. I was wearing jeans and an old T-shirt and as I glanced at Helen and Gabby I hoped that I looked a bit more presentable and smelt a bit better than they did.

As I stood there, I did once again wonder what on earth I was doing. I found I was able to answer the questions that were fired at us. Who were we? What church were we a part of? Why were we visiting? What did our mission do? The questions continued and I would reply. Gabby translated into Romanian and then his answers would be translated into Russian and discussed. After a while of questioning the atmosphere changed in the room and it all became friendlier. We discovered that we were speaking to the leadership of the Pentecostal Union of Evangelical Churches and were welcomed, accepted and offered a meal and accommodation.[9]

That evening Gabby and I shared a room with a man called Timofei. Timofei was a pastor from a church in the south who

9 Many of the brothers who were there in that room in June 1995 became dear friends over the following years. (As indeed have leaders from the Baptist Union also). I quite understand now why they were so wary of us at the beginning. At that time so few people were visiting Moldova and with strange new sects beginning to enter the new Soviet countries it was important for Evangelical church leaders to be cautious of who they welcomed into the country and worked with.

was working in Chisinau during the week. He invited us to visit his family and church at the weekend. Our list of contacts included people towards the south of the country and so we agreed to see him in a few days.

As we drove south the next day, I did once again question a little what we were actually planning to do there in Moldova. We had the name of someone called Victor from the village of Gura Galbanei. He had visited Romania at some stage, and met some of our friends there, and so he had made it onto our list. I had found some old maps of the Soviet Union and we used them to try and navigate around the country. One problem was that the clever authorities in Moscow had not included some of the main roads on their Soviet-era maps and had deliberately placed airports and some key towns in the wrong places so as to confuse any invading armies (or travelling missionaries). Also, many of the towns had only recently changed their names back to Moldovan names after the Soviet times and so navigating was a constant challenge – although Helen would always just shout turn right any time she sensed we were close to Nuremberg!

As we arrived in Gura Galbanei we realised we had a problem. We went to the centre of the dusty village and Gabby asked a little boy where Victor lived. The boy claimed to be Victor and it was then we realised that Victor was a very common name in Moldova. This was going to be harder than we had thought. We had not been able to phone or contact Victor in advance as we did not know his surname or address but had just prayed that morning that we would be able to find him and somehow be a blessing to him and his family. Someone eventually pointed us in the direction of the house of 'Victor the Christian', and we found it and parked our van outside a small village house.

A middle-aged couple came out of the gate and greeted us. Before we could explain who we were, we were ushered into the home. We were surprised to see a table set with three places – as if they knew we were coming. Sitting down we tried to explain who we were and could not understand how this couple seemed to have been expecting us. After much excited talking between Gabby and the couple we learnt that Tania, Victor's wife had dreamt the previous night that a white van with a green stripe, (exactly the van we were driving), would arrive at their home. She awoke knowing that they would be receiving guests that day. Tania had been killing chickens and preparing food all morning and we enjoyed a tasty meal and fellowship with this wonderful couple and their small children. Having prayed together and left them clothes, food and Christian books and tracts to distribute in the village, we drove on; marvelling at the way God had prepared the way for us.

The next days were spent in Gagauzia, a Turkic speaking region in southern Moldova. In this area it was even more difficult for us to communicate, as very few people spoke Romanian/Moldovan[10]. Still, we were received warmly everywhere we went and as we travelled we distributed aid, literature in Romanian and Russian and tasted wonderful Moldovan hospitality.

We had agreed to meet Timofei in Cahul, a city in the south. Arriving in the centre of the town we realised that it was not going to be easy to find him. However, as we sat in our van and prayed, a car pulled up and some men told us to follow them. We followed and soon arrived in a narrow, dusty street outside a typical Moldovan house – and there was Timofei. We were welcomed warmly by Jenya, his wife, and were able to talk and learn more about life for Christians in Moldova. Helen laughed when I told her that to get to the toilet you go past the dog, turn right at the chickens, continue on past the rabbits and pigs and stop just be-

10 Whilst Romanian is now the official state language of Moldova, there were times in the 1990s when officially the language was said to be Moldovan. Basically Moldovan is Romanian spoken with a different accent -with 'Moldovan colloquialisms' and quite a few words borrowed from Russian.

fore the cow and the goat. She laughed – until she returned from the outdoor toilet – and realised I had not been exaggerating!

Timofei was from a family who had been believers during communism and he and his wife shared with us about the fears, persecution and secret church meetings that had taken place in private homes during the Soviet times. That evening he took us to the local Baptist church where I was asked to preach. I had a couple of simple messages prepared and was able to speak with Gabby as translator. After the service people seemed encouraged. I received lots of kisses from the brothers who took the scriptural command literally to "greet each other with a holy kiss". As I puckered up, I saw the shock on Gabby's face – not for the first time on this trip – as men lined up to also kiss him on the lips, despite his desperate offer of a hand-shake.

As we were falling asleep that night in Timofei's house there was a knock on the door. Timofei came in and explained that we had guests. Gabby and I quickly dressed and Helen joined us from her room and a line of ten young ladies all dressed beautifully in skirts and head-scarfs came into our room. Timofei explained that this was the youth group and for the next couple of hours we talked with them about our faith, our churches and life in the West. They had so many questions. One girl, Tania, said to us, "I heard that in England people keep dogs in their homes … that's disgusting!" We had never really thought about this but realised just how different life was in Moldova compared with England. It was these sort of meetings that really helped us to begin to understand more of what life was like for people in Moldova and just how little contact people had with the West in those days.

Most people we visited were extremely poor. There was very little Western investment in the country and the majority of people tried to survive by growing their own food in their gardens. People would receive two lei (about fifty pence) for a day's work in the fields and bread cost eighty bani (20 pence). There were no Western-style shops where you served yourself. We had to point to what we wanted and it was taken down from a shelf and handed to us. Abacuses were used as calculators and change was rarely given. We found that if we paid 1 lei for bread, for example, instead of receiving change we would receive a cut slice from another loaf, or a box of matches or chewing gum.

Despite the obvious poverty and suffering we were looked after incredibly well. People often gave up their beds and precious food and always went out of their way to make us feel welcome and comfortable. The hospitality we received was incredibly humbling, as we often found ourselves sleeping in the children's beds as they shared with their parents; and eating the families' food when we knew that many of our hosts were struggling to provide for themselves. We helped every family we stayed with by giving food and clothes brought from Austria but we wished we could do more. Despite the obvious poverty, it seemed that the believers that we visited on that first trip were in so many ways richer than many people who have lots of possessions in the West. One man said to me, "we may be poor, but I would rather be poor and know Jesus, than be rich and not know him".

It was with a sense of awe, excitement and not a little relief that we arrived home to Austria and reported back to the team about our experiences. As we pulled into the office complex we were met by the OM Field Leader. He was excited to see us, and looking at Helen's hair commented that she must have been quick to take a shower, having only just arrived. Helen pointed out that what he thought was water on her hair was actually grease and that we had not seen running water for two weeks and not had an opportunity to wash for days!

Despite the challenges, the tiredness and the long journey we were bubbling over with enthusiasm. We had visited Moldova, the country that we had dreamt about for so long. We had seen

God working in and through us, opening doors and answering prayers, sometimes in quite miraculous ways. Something significant had happened in our hearts during that summer. We knew that sometime we would return to Moldova, but we had no idea then what that little country – hidden away in the corner of Europe – was going to come to mean to us in our lives in the future … but for now we had a wedding to prepare!

CHAPTER EIGHT

But Can He Really Provide For Me?

One of the challenges about working with a mission organisation such as OM is that no one receives a salary. In fact everyone needs to raise their own support in order to work. Basically you have to pay your own way by finding churches and friends who believe in your calling and the work you are doing. Support is sent in to the national OM office and it is forwarded to the field where you are serving. When you are a young person straight out of college, with not a penny to your name, and limited contacts, this can be particularly difficult. Few people really like asking other people for money and it is rarely easy for missionaries, having to write prayer letters and communicate with people the constant need for support.

I sensed God's calling to serve on the mission field but seriously doubted that I would be able to raise the money that was needed. Who would give money for me to be a missionary? As a single person I needed several hundreds of pounds each month for my support. My church agreed to help provide some, my parents seemed pleased that their son was going off to do something good and were very generous in their support and some individual church members also were very supportive and excited to see a young person who had grown up in their church heading off onto the mission field.

Still, in that first year with OM, I doubted that I would be able to last long under this sort of support system. I also knew, that as a married person on the mission field, the costs and support needs would be so much higher. Helen and I would need to rent an apartment and our all-round living costs would raise significantly. I was also very aware that within a year we were supposed to be getting married and we needed money for the wedding. Our parents had generously offered to cover most of the wedding expenses – for which we were extremely grateful – yet there were many other expenses surrounding the wedding and I was living in Austria, serving with OM, with no opportunity for earning money.

With this need for finances weighing on my mind I was sent on my first trip to Romania. Jana, an American lady, who had been responsible for OM's distribution of Christian literature in Romania was moving to Ukraine and, I, as the new recruit was to be taking over her job. Karin, the young lady, who later on that trip was to pray about Helen and me serving in Moldova also accompanied us as we set out on a journey to visit editors, publishers and book distributors.

We had packed the large OM van with literature, humanitarian aid and camping-gear and had left early in the morning from the base in Austria. The first day we drove all through Hungary and entered Romania late in the afternoon. The border guards searched the van suspiciously asking if we had guns or drugs; but after some time they lost interest and we were allowed to pass. We drove past old broken-down factories, along terribly pot-holed roads and through almost deserted streets lined by old high-rise Eastern European apartment blocks. We were in Transylvania, and, as the road started to wind up through the mountains, we stopped for our evening meal. I had bought bread, cheese and orange juice on our way through Hungary but as we bit into the sandwiches we realised that I had made a mistake. I had bought bread which was full of peppers and my sandwich and evening meal were ruined. I was pretty frustrated with myself for choosing the wrong bread. Even though I was hungry I could not stomach the bread and as it was already late there was no shops open where we could buy more. I started to realise just how uncomfortable a night was ahead of us. I was hungry and started to feel fed up. We were supposed to sleep in the van that night with the girls in the back and me lying in my sleeping-bag across the front seats. I knew I was not going to have a good night's sleep and, as we drove on looking for a place to park up for the night, I began to feel sorry for myself. I mean what is this all about? Is this really what missionaries have to go through? Sleeping on the front seat of a van in some strange country, uncomfortable and hungry! I knew that I had committed myself to following and serving God; "If it costs me everything ...", but did *everything* really have to include an uncomfortable bed and no proper food? I would finish this year of mission work and then go home, marry Helen and live happily ever after and not have to think any more about missions again – I would have done my year for God and I would be able to go home and start living a normal life! Surely that would be enough for God!?

As we drove around a corner a man motioned for us to stop. He was acting out that he needed a pump and so we pulled in. I took our foot pump from under my seat and approached the man and his small van to help him. As we took it in turns to pump up his tyre, he tried to speak to me but I knew hardly any Romanian at that stage and just smiled and nodded. We finished inflating the tyre. I had a Christian brochure in my pocket and gave it to him, picked up my pump and started back to our van. I was a little concerned as he grabbed my sleeve and motioned for me to follow him to the back of his van. I approached cautiously as he opened the back doors and I peered inside. There were shelves built into the interior of his van and they were filled with bread. He took a huge loaf out and handed it to me, thanked me for helping him and closed up the doors.

As I walked back to our van juggling the huge, still warm, loaf of bread I could hardly believe what had just happened. I climbed back into our van and showed off the bread to the girls and shared with them how I had been so frustrated because I was hungry and didn't have any proper bread. We ripped apart the delicious bread and together with hunks of cheese ate the most delicious 'sandwiches' I had ever tasted. That night, as I lay awake across the seats trying to avoid the gear stick, I heard once again an ever familiar Voice. Again, inaudible, yet as clear as if someone were sitting next to me and speaking; "Matthew, do you see? You do not need to worry about anything. I can provide for all your needs. Nothing is too difficult for me; you just need to learn to trust me!"

I have often thought about that moment, when for the first time I really saw that the words of Jesus are true, "Seek first the kingdom of God and my righteousness – and I will take care of the rest" (my slight paraphrase of Matthew 6:33). Over the years our faith in the God who can provide for all our needs has often been tested, but we have come to learn that He truly is a God who provides for all of our needs; our challenge so often is learning to trust Him.

I was reminded again of this truth a few months later when Helen and I, plus our chaperone, were travelling again in the mountains or Romania. It was getting late and we were looking for a safe place to park up and sleep for the night. We turned a corner and saw a beautiful spot; green grass, next to a small river, slightly hidden from the road. It was perfect apart from the fact that it was on the other side of the river and just a small, rickety looking wooden bridge separated us from the ideal camping spot.

I got out of the van and walked onto the bridge stamping my feet, which I knew was a particularly pointless and futile thing to do, but it made me feel better. The wood underfoot showed signs of rot in parts but seemed fairly sturdy. We were both unsure as to whether the bridge would take the weight of our van but we were tired and decided that we would risk it. Before starting across the bridge in our three-and-a-half ton van, I suggested Helen get out and walk across. It wasn't that I was suggesting that she added significantly to the weight, just that I thought that if the van was to plunge into the river, then we didn't both need to be inside. So Helen walked across the bridge and I revved the engine and gripping the steering-wheel harder than ever. I floored the accelerator, somehow thinking that we would be lighter if we moved faster. I am sure I felt the bridge creek and move as I shot across, but we made it and started setting up camp, trying not to think that the next morning we would need to make the crossing back in the opposite direction.

As Helen prepared some soup to go with our sandwiches, I collected up wood to make a fire to keep the bears away. As I returned to the river and loaded up with wood I heard a rumbling noise and saw a huge logging-truck approaching. Obviously the men on board had been at work all day as the truck was loaded with around a dozen, twenty metre (66ft) long logs. The truck, which must have weighed at least ten times more than our van, trundled up and over the bridge and continued on up the mountain track. As I stood there I smiled to myself feeling pretty silly at the thought of our fear when crossing the bridge. We didn't need to have any fear, for that bridge could support our weight easily. A familiar voice whispered a question, "What is the difference between you and the other driver Matthew?" I realised immediately that the other driver knew the bridge; he knew that it was strong; he knew that it could easily hold his weight, and he had absolute trust and faith in that bridge. I stood there and thought about my relationship with God. It was as if He were saying: "Matthew I am more than strong enough, I can carry you, I can provide for you – do you trust me? If you really knew me you would trust me!"

The journey back across the bridge the next morning was worry-free. We laughed as we crossed, even with Helen's extra weight in the van, for we now knew the bridge could easily support us.

After that first year serving with OM in Eastern Europe, we returned to England in the autumn of 1995 to prepare for our wedding. We were struggling financially. Our parents were paying for pretty much everything but we did not feel we could ask them also for money for the honeymoon, so, not having any other options, we realised we needed to pray. We really liked the idea of going to a place that was hot, but it was November and that would mean travelling outside Europe – and we had no money! We did not feel it was right to ask people for money for this. Many friends had supported me on the mission field the previous year. Our parents were already being very generous with the wedding expenses and so we were left with no option but to pray – and see what God would do. We didn't *have* to go somewhere exotic for our honeymoon but wondered if God would somehow provide for us and bless us. Without telling anyone that we needed money and within days of us starting to pray specifically for money for a honeymoon, around five-hundred pounds had been given to us by friends or in envelopes anonymously appearing on the doorstep. God was providing and we were going to have an amazing honeymoon! We headed to the travel agency thinking that it would be wonderful to go somewhere hot and sunny, if our budget permitted. When we saw that holidays in Sri Lanka were just about within budget we took the decision. We paid the deposit and looked forward to spending 10 days at the two-star Emerald Bay holiday resort. A week later we had to pay the remaining sum and were trusting that God would provide for us in time. As the deadline day approached we had other expenses of buying a suit and shoes and other essentials for the big day. As we counted our money we realised that we were one hundred and twenty-five pounds short. We didn't have enough to pay for the honeymoon! We really did not feel that we could ask anyone to lend us the money but had no idea what to do other than pray and ask for a miracle. The day arrived when we had to pay the remaining sum for the holiday. I awoke early and I have to admit, that despite my efforts to remain super-spiritual, my morning quiet time was dominated by my concern about the money. It certainly crossed my mind that God may do a miracle and money might arrive through the post and so when I heard the postman putting a letter through the front door I ran quickly to see what had arrived. I half expected to open a letter from some long lost friend who just happened to be prompted by God to send us money! This was it; God was going to do a miracle and we would get to have a great honeymoon in Sri Lanka … but no! The only letter was from the tourist agency, an unnecessary reminder that I needed to pay the remaining sum that day. I opened the letter and glanced through the text. It was an unusual letter. The agency expressed deep regret and informed us that due to escalating problems between Tamil Tigers and government forces in Sri Lanka there had to be changes in our booking. We could still go on our holiday but the cost had changed and we were being offered the same holiday but at a discount of … ONE HUNDRED AND TWENTY FIVE POUNDS! I could hardly believe what I was reading, does this ever happen? Surely this was no coincidence, and as I phoned Helen and told her the news we both realised afresh that we had a God who cared for us and could provide for all our needs. We were about to begin our lives together as husband and wife and we were in awe of what God was doing. He was really present in our lives. He really seemed to be providing for us, blessing us, seemingly smiling upon us and delighting in us. We just had to learn to walk more closely with Him, to learn to trust Him more, for we realised that nothing, absolutely nothing was too difficult for Him.

And so on the 4th November 1995, on a beautiful autumn day, I finally married the girl who had played such a significant role in transforming my life. We made our vows and exchanged rings in my home church, Ashley Baptist. Inside our wedding rings we had had engraved words from the Bible, Jeremiah 29:11 …

'For I know the plans I have for you', declares the Lord, 'plans to prosper you and not to harm you, plans to give you hope and a future.'

These words had become a special promise for us. We felt they were particularly relevant for us beginning our married life together on the mission field and reminding us constantly of God's love, provision and blessing.

After our amazing honeymoon in Sri Lanka we returned to England and spent a month house-sitting for a family from our church. During that time we lived mainly on apples that we picked from the back garden and we both began Theology degrees by correspondence – which we felt was important for us if we were to continue in ministry longer term. We spent the rest of our time studying Romanian and preparing for returning to Austria. A month later, on 28th December 1995, we packed the Ashley church minibus with all of our wedding presents and some old furniture and set off for Austria with Adam and his girlfriend, Pip – turning right at Nuremberg! We settled into our rented apartment in the village of Grossmugl, north of Vienna, and were ready to begin the next chapter of our 'missionary adventure'.

CHAPTER NINE
East of Austria

We returned excitedly to the OM Greater Europe team in Austria, with a two-year commitment, and with plans to continue to develop the work of producing and distributing literature in Romania. We had also been asked to take over leading evangelistic outreach-teams into Ukraine; but our passion was increasingly for Moldova and we hoped to begin some sort of ministry there also.

For the next two years we lived in Grossmugl, a small village north of Vienna. However, we never really settled into Austrian life as we spent six months of the year outside Austria travelling in Eastern Europe. We were young, we were excited and full of energy and we threw ourselves into our ministry with gusto.

We had so many adventures during those first two years as a married couple. In twenty-five trips into Eastern Europe our van broke down fifteen times! In the days before mobile phones we often found ourselves hitching lifts, trying to explain mechanical problems in German, Hungarian, Romanian, Ukrainian or Russian; and learned never to drive anywhere without duct tape and wire coat-hangers, which we discovered could be used to fix a variety of mechanical problems.

We learnt how to export literature and aid from the EU, how to negotiate contracts with printers in Romania, persuade border guards to work, discuss with policemen wanting bribes, rescue horses from rivers, fit snow-chains, drive on ice, work cross-culturally, sing in different languages, sleep in vans in freezing temperatures, minister to orphans, establish sales networks of Christian books, preach and share our testimonies in many different situations. Above all, we experienced daily how God was leading us, answering prayers and clearly confirming to us that we were doing what He wanted us to do!

As we drove heavy vans, loaded with literature around Eastern Europe, we saw dozens of accidents. One day, we watched as a van in front of us lost control, and slid off the road and disappeared down a steep bank. It was always sobering seeing bodies removed from cars that had crashed ahead of us on the road, and we were constantly reminded about just how fragile life was and how much we were depending upon the Lord for protection.

One memorable journey, our brakes failed as we drove our three-ton van, loaded with Christian books down the famous Trans-Fagaras, Romanian mountain road. The road stretches ninety kilometres and crosses the tallest sections of the southern Carpathians making it one of the highest, most spectacular, but also most dangerous roads in Europe. We had camped on the top of the mountain and as we drove away the next morning I touched the brake pedal and was shocked to realise that nothing was happening! Our speed was not too great so I was able to slow down by going through the gears and pulled to the side of the road with the hand-brake just before a sharp bend and a barrierless, hundred metre drop. We drove very gingerly the rest of the way down the mountain.

Despite the challenges of poor quality roads, dangerous mountain passes, snow and ice, there was a constant sense that the Lord was protecting and looking after us. It was quite remarkable that we were kept from any accidents during those travelling years.

One Saturday when we had a day off in Austria, I, together with two friends, Roger and Doug decided to try and climb a mountain just south of Vienna. It was a fresh, autumn morning and we set off early, so as to have time to get up and down the mountain before dark. There was snow in the air and it was beginning to settle lightly on the autobahn as we took the ring-road around Vienna and headed south. As we drove tentatively, a car passed us in the outside lane and then we watched in horror as it pulled in front of us and began to lose control. It veered one way and the other as the driver fought in vain to hold a straight line. Almost in slow motion the car turned sideways still moving at around eighty kilometres (fifty miles) per hour. We continued in our lane, braking slightly as we bore down on the car that was now travelling just ahead of us but sideways. I saw the look of terror on the face of the man as he gripped the steering wheel just metres in front of our car. Suddenly, the car was swept out of our lane, and crashed spectacularly against the crash-barrier on the hard shoulder, facing the wrong direction. We pulled in and saw the man getting out of his car shaken but unharmed. We continued our journey realising just how close we had come to crashing, but also aware that it was somehow miraculous that we had not ploughed into the side of the other car. It really was as if something or someone had simply swept the other car out of our path at the very last moment.

We had a fun but tiring day out in the mountains and headed home, driving especially carefully. On arriving back in our apartment, the phone rang. It was Karen a young American lady also serving on the OM mission team. She asked us what had happened at 08.20 that morning. Slightly taken aback I asked her why she wanted to know. She said that she had been having a lie in and was just getting up when she had felt an overwhelming urge to pray for our safety. She explained that this sort of thing did not usually happen to her but she just knew that we were in some sort of danger and she told how she had knelt and prayed fervently for our protection. We realised that God had prompted Karen to pray for us at exactly the time that we had been so close to having an accident!

I had lots of questions. I knew that God had protected us from having an accident that could have been serious, yet there was so much I did not understand. Why had He prompted Karen to pray for us at that time? Would it have worked if she had prayed the evening before? Was an angel involved, protecting us from the accident? Did I really believe in angels and how did they work? What did they look like? Did God need someone to be praying for us in order for Him to work? Couldn't He just have protected us anyway? Why did He work in this way for us and yet allow others to suffer and die in accidents? So many questions, yet there was one underlying certainty – God was protecting us and looking after us. Our lives were truly in His hands and we knew there was no safer place to be.

In those early years based in Austria, during our first years of married life, we travelled and ministered and constantly sensed God's hand of blessing, provision and protection upon us. It was as if God were smiling, and saying, "Matthew, do you still think that trusting and walking with me is boring?" I was learning that 'abundant life' really was only found when we follow Jesus, and I often remembered back to my former doubts about where to find true life.

I have come that you may have life and life in abundance (John 10 :10).

———————

It was not always easy and those years were filled with blessings but also challenges. In the spring of 1995 within days of Helen joining the team in Austria, together with Karin from Sweden, we packed the van with aid and literature and headed for Romania. I was excited to introduce my fiancée to the people I had started to work with. Helen was also excited to be with me serving on the mission field after having spent the best part of the previous twelve months in different countries. Helen's excitement however was short-lived. Her first trip with me in Romania was quite a baptism of fire.

After leaving Austria early and crossing Hungary, we entered Romania and the first night we slept in the van high in the mountains in Transylvania. Helen and Karin rearranged the boxes of books and made beds in the back of the van for themselves, and I again had to negotiate the gear stick whilst trying to sleep across the front seats. We all had two sleeping-bags but it was still freezing-cold and when I awoke stiff from the cold in the morning I was worried to discover that I couldn't move my head! I quickly realised that my woolly hat that I was wearing had frozen to window and so I carefully removed my head from it before ripping it free from the ice-covered glass. I could see my breath, but little else, as thick ice had formed on the inside of the windows. There was silence from the rear of the van and I wondered how Helen and Karin had fared during the night. Snow had been falling through the night and as I awoke the girls we all realised just how cold it was. Our orange juice cartons had frozen solid during the night and so we built a small fire, melted some ice and made some tea. Thankfully, the van started as we had added 'helicopter fuel' to the diesel, which prevented it from freezing at below –18 C (0 F). We scraped the ice from the windows and continued our journey to the city of Brasov in order to deliver books to shops and publishers there.

It wasn't until later that day that I began to realise how challenging the whole experience was becoming for Helen. We had stopped just south of Brasov at Bran Castle, famously known as Dracula's home. The snow was getting deeper and we realised we needed snow-chains fitted before continuing the journey south, to the city of Pitesti. As I lay under the van and fought the chains with frozen fingers Helen gallantly tried passing me tools and offering advice and encouragement. Suddenly I felt something warm and wet pushing against my face and I was shocked to feel a hairy animal pushing up against me as I lay half under the van. Bears and wolves were commonly seen in that part of Romania and I panicked and hit my head as I tried to quickly slide out from under the van and fight off whatever it was that had tried to attack me under the van. Helen shooed off the 'wolf', which she claimed was only a stray dog and after fitting the chains we entered a local restaurant to try and warm up. The restaurant boasted an impressive menu but in reality only had cabbage soup and pork cutlets on offer. So there we sat, eating our soup and wondering what we had let ourselves in for.

As I sat opposite Helen I saw tears in her eyes. Karin wisely decided to go for a walk and I looked at Helen and wondered what I could say to try and encourage her. She had been the one who had always spoken about feeling called to serve on the mission field, so it wasn't my fault that we were here! We had spent the last year or so apart as we each undertook the Discipleship Training Schools with YWAM. Now, here we were, finally on the mission field together; travelling in Transylvania, freezing in an uncomfortable van at night, fighting off wild dogs in Dracula's Castle and eating cabbage soup in a dirty restaurant – real missionary life! It was not exactly what Helen had signed up for when she had committed her life to serve God on the mission field as a fifteen-year old at a Spring Harvest Christian Conference!

I looked at Helen and realised that there was nothing I could say to actually encourage her. Sometimes things do not go smoothly, life can be tough, and however much I can be tempted to try and explain and justify and advise, I have learnt that often it is best to just keep quiet, listen and not try to 'fix' other people – especially my wife! It sounds simple but it is of course not always easy, especially when sitting outside Dracula's castle having been attacked by wild dogs.

I really seemed to be being challenged about patience (or rather my impatience) during those journeys. We stopped in one village to buy bread and whilst Helen went into a small store, I waited impatiently in the van, engine running, aware that we were late for our next appointment. Helen soon returned and made up cheese sandwiches and passed them to me as I drove. I wolfed them down and also hungrily devoured a cream pastry that she had passed on to me. It tasted a bit funny and left quite a taste in my mouth, but, it wasn't until Helen finished her sandwiches and began her pastry that she cried out in disgust. The cream in the pastry had gone off and was green! She actually showed me the green cream oozing horribly from between mouldy pastry which probably dated from the time of Ceausescu's rule. It was then that I really started to feel ill! What had I just eaten? What had Helen just fed me? Why had I been in such a rush to gulp down my food? The phrase 'the early bird gets the worm but the second mouse gets the cheese' had never been truer. As I drove, feeling sicker and sicker, I realised that it was not always wise to rush – and that perhaps I needed to learn to be a little more patient with myself and others.

We completed our trip and returned to Austria realising that missionary life was not always going to be easy. But, we had survived the 'wolves' in Dracula's Castle and were ready for the next challenge. (Okay, so it probably wasn't actually a wolf but by the time we got back to Austria the dog may have become slightly more wolf-like in our minds when we retold the story!)

Our outreaches to Ukraine were always challenging but at the same time very exciting. We would spend months in contact with OM offices around the world trying to recruit people to join us on the outreach. Then, there was the lining up and communication with receiving churches in Ukraine which was all of course done without email, through poor telephone lines trying to communicate with people speaking different languages. There was also the preparation time with new recruits when they arrived in Austria, the packing of the bus with aid and literature, the long drive across Hungary, arguing with customs officials and border crossings that sometimes lasted twenty four hours, police check-points, break-downs, and problems with the KGB or secret police.

In 1996 we were working with a small church in the town of Kazatin, Ukraine. The local security authorities were very suspicious of foreigners, and followed us around for days, before finally taking us in for questioning. As the team-leader, I found myself standing before different uniformed and armed officials as they asked endless questions about our motives for being in their town. It was at times intimidating for me as a twenty-four year old trying to answer the questions being fired at me – but I had nothing to hide and so shared my faith with everyone I could. One man was clearly trained in interrogation techniques and was so friendly at the beginning, building a rapport with me, even showing some interest in the Gospel message, before suddenly changing and threatening me with arrest and deportation if I did not take the team and leave his town. Now, with hindsight and more experience, I realise that seventy years of communist propaganda did not disappear from people's minds overnight, and there was a very real fear of the West and what we as foreigners were really doing in their country. There was also always the suggestion that 'a few American Dollars' could resolve any problem, and we constantly faced ethical challenges to know what was, and was not, the right way to proceed in a whole host of different situations.

Despite the constant problems with local authorities, everywhere we went we always had wonderful opportunities and open doors to share the hope that we have in Christ: whether in orphanages, kindergartens, hospitals, schools, market-places, parks, bus and train stations – as well, of course, in churches.

The goal for these outreaches was to mobilise people from other countries to join us for a life changing missions experience, share our faith with as many people as possible *and* to encourage local believers in their faith in whatever way we were able. In Kazatin, the whole church of twelve people, joined us on our bus as we drove from place to place, (followed by the rather conspicuous KGB officer in his little Russian car). One day, as we drove, Helen was preparing food for the team in the back of the bus. She called to me and explained that we did not have enough sandwiches for everyone. There was only enough for our team of twelve, but with the local believers also with us, we simply did not have enough to go around for everyone. We were in a fairly remote place on the way to share our faith in a tuberculosis hospital. There were no shops around and people were looking to me as the team-leader to know what to do. We decided to simply share out what we had, gave thanks and hoped that it would be enough to keep us going. My prayer in English in front of the team and the non-English speaking Ukrainian church members was something like; "Dear Lord, thank you for this good food, please help us as the team to be willing to hold back and not eat as much so that our hosts can eat enough first … hint, hint … Amen." It was not really a prayer – more an announcement to the team to hold back. Just as I finished 'praying' the driver stopped the bus to ask for directions. A *babushka,* (old lady), came to the steps of the bus. She was carrying a plate of cheese and salami sandwiches and another plate of chopped tomatoes and cucumbers. Rick, the driver, opened the door and one of the translators asked her directions to the hospital as she handed the plates to the people in the front seats. She pointed us in the right direction, climbed down from the bus and left! Some people more spiritually-minded than me would perhaps claim that this lady was an angel sent by God! I however looked at her old, wizened face and missing teeth, and reckoned that God would surely make His angels a little better-looking. But, I couldn't argue with what had just happened – there she had appeared, on the steps of our bus with sandwiches and salad and we thanked her, thanked God and all ate well. We travelled on to the hospital to share our faith and hope, to people who were suffering and dying from tuberculosis, having been reminded once again, that God was in control of all things. We continued to be so encouraged and blessed during what were always exciting, and very often challenging times. I often heard the Voice whispering "I love you, Matthew. I can provide for you – do you trust me? Are you really willing to step out and live by faith?"

I did not consider myself to be a particularly great preacher, but I was becoming more experienced and learning how to speak effectively through a translator. There were times, as I prepared messages back in Austria to preach in Romania, Ukraine or Moldova that I really sensed God leading me to a particular passage or text. I would often feel a peace and sense of assurance that God would use my simple messages to speak to people about their relationship with Him. After one Gospel meeting, a young man in his thirties came to speak with me. He was clearly touched by the message and wanted to pray to God, ask forgiveness for his sins and begin a new life in relationship with God through His Son Jesus Christ. As we prayed together, I sensed, and saw from the tears in his eyes, that God really seemed to have met with and touched this man in a special way. Over the following days Tudor accompanied us and even began sharing his new faith with other people as we ministered in different

Matthew David joins the family in March 1972

The rabbit is definitely over there

I always was better than Adam at football

Adam and me – 1978

The famous Vale Middle School football team
with the first school right back still holding the ball

The beginning of the OM Moldova River Outreach? Summer holiday 1980

Resting with Dad in the middle of a family hike

Hiking, climbing and boating nurtured a spirit of adventure that has remained with me

The girl with the green Doc Martin boots

She caused all the problems
by constantly talking about missions

On the infamous balcony in Ufa
Baptist church, Russia

With Neville and his sister –
just before we killed the crocodile

...LALUNI

Engagement in 1994

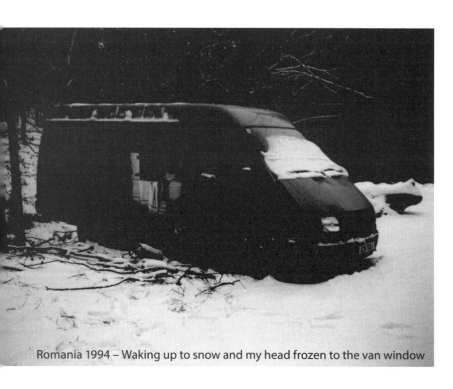
Romania 1994 – Waking up to snow and my head frozen to the van window

Fitting snow chains in Romania 1994 –
just before the 'wolf' attacked

Our first trip to Moldova – June 1995

Wedding Day –
November 4th 1995

The first OM evangelistic team to work in Moldova. September 1996

Cojusna 1997 – just before a drunk man decided to attack us

Preaching in the fields in Transnistria –
the police did not have money to pay for petrol to come and stop us

Using a rope illustration to share the Gospel – Gotesti, Cahul, 1996

Always trying to keep warm – Nisporeni 1998

The growing youth group – Nisporeni 1999

The first OM Moldova Team – Nisporeni 1998–1999

One of the first Challenge into Missions Teams on the final outreach – with the Logos II in St Petersburg, Russia, with baby Hanna – Spring 2001

LOGOS II

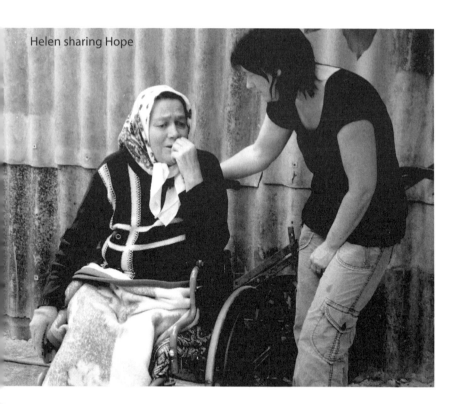

Helen sharing Hope

Rachel, David, James, Hanna and Lydia on the river outreach

Preaching in a house church in Vanator, Nisporeni

Helen handing out biscuits to children at −15 °C

OM Moldova Team 2004

OM Moldova team 2014

Skirton family 2013

Still laughing after 23 years of married life in Moldova

Skirton family 2014

Matthew David joins the family in March 1972

The rabbit is definitely over there

I always was better than Adam at football

Adam and me – 1978

The famous Vale Middle School football team
with the first school right back still holding the ball

Resting with Dad in the middle of a family hike

The beginning of the OM Moldova River Outreach? Summer holiday 1980

Hiking, climbing and boating nurtured a spirit of adventure that has remained with me

The girl with the green Doc Martin boots

She caused all the problems
by constantly talking about missions

On the infamous balcony in Ufa
Baptist church, Russia

With Neville and his sister –
just before we killed the crocodile

Engagement in 1994

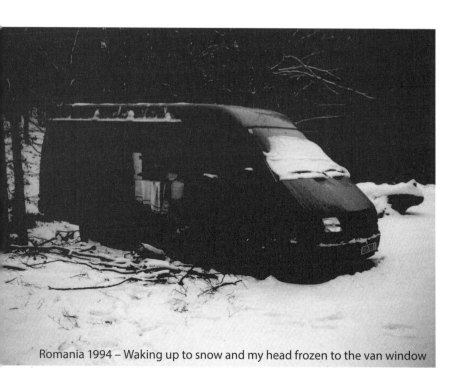

Romania 1994 – Waking up to snow and my head frozen to the van window

Fitting snow chains in Romania 1994 –
just before the 'wolf' attacked

Our first trip to Moldova – June 1995

Wedding Day –
November 4th 1995

The first OM evangelistic team to work in Moldova. September 1996

Cojusna 1997 – just before a drunk man decided to attack us

Preaching in the fields in Transnistria –
the police did not have money to pay for petrol to come and stop us

Using a rope illustration to share the Gospel – Gotesti, Cahul, 1996

Always trying to keep warm – Nisporeni 1998

The growing youth group – Nisporeni 1999

The first OM Moldova Team – Nisporeni 1998–1999

One of the first Challenge into Missions Teams on the final outreach – with the Logos II in St Petersburg, Russia, with baby Hanna – Spring 2001

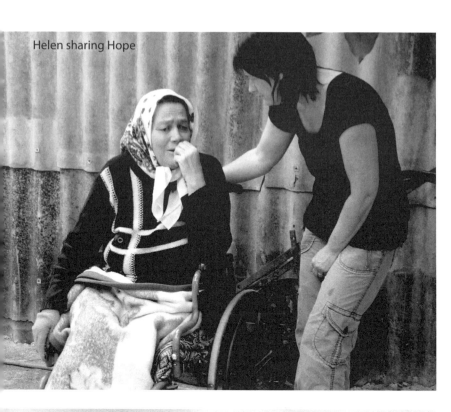

Helen sharing Hope

Rachel, David, James, Hanna and Lydia
on the river outreach

Preaching in a house church
in Vanator, Nisporeni

Helen handing out biscuits
to children at −15 °C

OM Moldova Team 2004

OM Moldova team 2014

Skirton family 2013

Still laughing after 23 years of married life in Moldova

Skirton family 2014

places. I saw in Tudor an excitement for God and his Word. It was clear that God had really done something in his life and he was bubbling over to tell others about the hope he now had.

We left Kazatin and began the long drive home. Tired, yet blessed and excited at how God had been working. I was encouraged. I had been doing the work of a missionary. Wow, Missionary, me! I knew the truth found in God's Word and had been active in sharing that truth with others. I was being used by God to bring the Good News to people who had never heard. I was a *real* missionary doing *real* missionary stuff! God had done miracles, He had answered prayers. He was with us – life was good! I was young, I was full of energy and zeal. I knew God and had seen how He was at work. My understanding of God however was about to be completely shaken.

After some weeks of being back in Austria, I began reading a book by the American theologian R. C. Sproul called 'The Holiness of God'. As I read, it seemed that my understanding of who God is got bigger and bigger. It was as if God Himself was opening my eyes to understand Him more. One day, as I was reading the book, I received a letter from our new friends in Ukraine and to my horror I learnt that Tudor had been killed in a terrible accident in the factory where he worked. I could not believe what I was reading. This was not right! How could God have allowed this to happen? I thought of Tudor's family; his wife who was not yet a believer and his seven-year old daughter, and I was shaken. The God I had come to believe in would not allow something like this to happen! I got on my knees with the book and letter on the floor before me, and with tears running down my face I cried out to God and said "Lord, I thought I knew you – how could you allow this to happen?" I was angry and confused. I wanted answers.

God was silent!

As I wept and struggled to understand how God could allow this, I reflected upon the message of the book I was reading. God is holy! He is holy! He is Lord, above all things. He has all things in control, He is holy! This did not give me an answer as to why Tudor had been allowed to die in such a horrific accident. However, as I got up from my knees, there was a sense that I was in the presence of One who was far above – and yet so close. I knew that He is God, He is in control and I am not and that is all right!

This may sound a bit funny and perhaps a little obvious, but I have found it amazing over the years how we who call ourselves Christians can so easily begin to think we know God and that He somehow exists exclusively for us. After all, we live 'in relationship with Him', we have 'invited Jesus into our hearts', God is our loving Father, our best friend and counsellor and He should of course do exactly what we want, when we want because we are after all Christians! I find that my understanding of God can so easily be reduced in my mind to Him being like a little puppy that I have on a lead, a sort of pet or lucky charm that I take around with me; a personal god, that I get used to carrying around, and that brings luck and prosperity in my life, before finally taking me up to heaven to be with Him forever. I find that not only I, but so many Christians that I meet, seem to at times fall into this false understanding of God; that He should always do what we want, when we want and we should always be able to understand Him and His workings.

Something significant happened in my heart that day – as I realised that yes, He is loving and kind and merciful and forgiving and a counsellor and friend and all of those things – but He is also holy. He is all powerful, all knowing, the Creator of the universe, Holy, Holy, Holy! He is … and I am not … and as I knelt in my bedroom, I wept as this profound understanding of the majesty and holiness of God took another step on its journey from my head to my heart.

Missionary, me? There I was the 'great missionary', beginning to preach and teach others about a God who, I had come to realise, I did not really know, and did not really understand. Years later I read CS Lewis' Narnia books. Aslan the lion, who is a picture of Christ, is described not as being *safe* but as being *good*, as being the King.[11] I read how later in the stories, Aslan tells the children that as they grow he also will appear to grow; and on that day, on my knees, in my room, I was struck by this revelation. God is real, He is good, He is the King but He is not particularly safe and He cannot be limited and placed in a box. The more I grow to understand Him, the closer I seem to get, yet the more I realise just how little of Him and His ways I really know and understand.

Missionary, me? – Yes! I was an evangelical Christian – a Christian missionary! I had invited Jesus into my heart and committed my life to him. I even knew by heart all the songs that good Christians should sing. Yet, within my Christianity, in the midst of my early years on the mission field, I had so personalised God that I had come to see Him somehow as *safe* and *tame*; existing to be at my beck and call, to do what I wanted and when I wanted it. Receiving the news about Tudor and kneeling alone in my room before a truly holy God changed me profoundly. From that day, my understanding of life and faith perhaps started to be just a little less monochrome. The God I prayed to, and told others about, had outgrown my simplistic evangelical mind. But maybe that was a good thing. Maybe as we walk with Him He is supposed to get bigger and bigger. Now, whenever I speak to God, when I dare to stand before people and speak *about* Him, the realisation sweeps over me again and again, He *is* and I am *not*, and this humbling truth often brings me to my knees.

11 CS Lewis, The Lion, the Witch & The Wardrobe

CHAPTER TEN

Cherries, Anyone?

"You might be a spy, you cannot enter our country!"

We had become accustomed to difficult border crossings and even threats by border officials, but this was different. The young soldiers were armed with Kalashnikovs and were thrilled to have some 'Amerikani' to hold and interrogate. We were trying to cross the river Nistru and enter Transnistria, a self-declared independent country that had not long before fought a six month war with Moldova. The Russian army had occupied this thin slither of Moldova and a 'president' and 'government' were seeking international recognition for their 'country'. The international community warned against foreigners travelling to Transnistria, and it was probably this, together with reports of persecution of Christians there, that increased our growing desire to make a visit to this country within a country.

Our trips into Romania and Ukraine always seemed to be filled with exciting challenges and we experienced God's provision and protection time and again as we travelled around Eastern Europe. It was however, Moldova that continued to really capture our imagination and draw us. There was a sense of inevitability that we would end up there and ever since our visit in June 1995 we had planned to return. We continued to build up a list of contacts throughout the country and in the summer of 1996 we were back, this time as a married couple. We had learned our lesson, and understood that both Romanian and Russia translation would be needed. So, a Romanian translator as well as a Ukrainian friend who had taken the train in to Chisinau, travelled with us. We thought we were ready for any and every translation eventuality – until we found ourselves in three Bulgarian villages.

Back in Austria, before the trip, the OM workers in Bulgaria had offered us their surplus stock of Bulgarian Christian literature. We had read in Operation World[12] that there were lots of ethnic Bulgarians in Moldova, and so together with humanitarian aid and Romanian and Russian Bibles and books, we also loaded up with boxes of Bulgarian Christian books, praying – "Please Lord lead us to some Bulgarians!"

After the three day, 1 500 kilometre (930 mile) drive, we again crossed the border into Moldova, still with a significant amount of fear and trepidation. We travelled to the south and revisited friends we had made the previous year. It was wonderful to be back in the country and amongst people that we were increasingly feeling burdened to do everything possible to serve.

After a visit to a village church, we stopped the van to tidy up and rearrange the boxes, which also acted as our bed at night. An elderly man approached us and began to tell us his story and how difficult his life was. We could see in his eyes a deep sadness, even hopelessness, and our hearts were moved. Helen quickly put together a packet of flour, sugar and rice with some Christian literature as I shared with him through our translator the hope that we have in Christ. His eyes filled with tears as he shared how he had turned away from God and the Church. I told him that God

12 A very helpful book that provides detailed information as well as important prayer requests for every country in the world. Operation World, by Jason Mandryk, InterVarsity Press

loved him and that he could find hope, forgiveness and a new life in Jesus. As we spoke he fell to his knees. I thought that somehow he was bowing down to us and went to stop him – then I heard him praying. There he was on his knees next to our van, on a dusty road in the middle of nowhere and he was repenting and crying out to God for forgiveness! His desperation and actions did not seem to be fuelled by alcohol as was too often the case. He really, genuinely seemed to have been touched by God right there in front of us. As we handed him the food packet and encouraged him to continue to seek God, he assured us that he would visit the local evangelical church. As we drove away I felt once again a deep confirmation in my spirit that God Himself had called us to do what we were seeking to do in this exciting new country.

And so it was, on that same trip, that we arrived at the border of Transnistria. The young soldiers were really suspicious, angry and intimidating. They shouted at us that we needed visas to enter *their* country and as they surrounded us I felt that perhaps it was not such a good idea to try and enter. It struck me that *leaving* Transnistria may prove to be even harder than entering; we knew we were entering a place that the UN and Western embassies advised against visiting.

After some time, and threats, and negotiations, and us promising to register with the local security services within three hours; we drove past the guards, bunkers and armoured vehicles, under the Soviet stars, hammer and sickles, past the large statue of Lenin, and headed to the local Pentecostal church. Could we really do something to help people in this intimidating, closed and depressing place? We were invited to the pastor's home and after a wonderful meal, we spent the afternoon on his terrace, eating cherries and learning more about this strange new 'country'.

The situation between Moldova and Transnistria was still very tense – even a couple of years after the war. The presence of Russian 'peacekeepers' was seen by the government in Chisinau as a hostile act, and the local authorities, with backing from Moscow, had established their own government, army and even currency. Poverty and inflation were high, with 90 million *Rouble Coupons* to the pound. Three extra zeros had just been printed onto local bank notes some weeks before we arrived. It was common to see people going to the market with a 'brick' of bank notes an inch thick just to buy some vegetables.

We chatted for most of the afternoon and towards the end of our discussion I noticed a worm in a cherry that I was eating. Throwing it away I took another cherry and found another worm. Opening more cherries, I realised that all the cherries contained worms – I had spent the last hour eating dozens and dozens of worms with my cherries. They had been delicious, but psychologically I was struggling and as we headed to the local church I increasingly began to feel unwell. We took part in the service, singing, sharing testimony and preaching, but with some sense of relief we finished the service. I received lots of holy kisses from the brothers, much to Helen's amusement, until the *babushkas* decided that she also needed kissing – on the lips! Then, a middle-aged lady called Olya approached us and invited us to her home. She said she had lots of cherries that she wanted to give us as a gift. The last thing I wanted to see again in my life was a cherry, so we declined her offer. She was however so insistent that in the end we accepted – but I assured myself that however impolite it may seem, there was no way I was going to eat another cherry that day.

We had a wonderful time of fellowship with Olya and managed graciously to receive a huge bag of cherries without having to eat any. As we were leaving, Olya happened to mention that she was not actually Moldovan or Russian, but she was Bulgarian. As soon as I heard this I said "Praise God, we have some books for you!" I asked her if she knew any other Bulgarians and she laughed. She said that the majority of the people in her village were Bulgarian and she taught Bulgarian at the local school. She wept as we told her of our prayers that we would meet Bulgarians and be able to give out the literature we had brought. We left Olya with boxes of Children's Bibles and other Christian books that she was able to then take to the school and give to the children.

As we drove away, we again thanked God for the way He was opening doors and leading us. We thanked Him as we managed to get back past the 'border guards' and return to Moldova, and we even thanked Him for the bag of cherries that Olya had given to us – although my stomach did grumble a bit that night.

Some days later I was on my knees crying out to God – "Oh Lord, what am I doing here?" I was one of hundreds of people kneeling and praying in a large church in the city of Balti. We had been travelling in the south and east of Moldova and were visiting a friend, Grigore, in his home church in Balti, towards the north. We had brought some books to the church but this church already had such a large congregation and I wondered if they really needed our help. Were we just wasting our time at this huge church?

One of our prayers back in Austria, before leaving, was that we would be able to make contact with churches in the north-east region of the country. We had started to develop contacts in the south, centre, Gagauz region and even Transnistria; but as I sat in my office in Austria and gazed at the map of Moldova on the wall, it was the north east that seemed particularly to draw my attention. Was it God speaking to me or just my imagination or sense of adventure, wanting to go to a new place? I prayed a simple prayer back in Austria – "Please Lord, if it is your will for us to visit the north east then open the doors and lead us to the right people."

After the service in Balti, where I had begun to question seriously what we were doing, we stood amongst the crowds and were introduced to a small, middle-aged man called Pavel. Pavel, it turned out, was a pastor and church planter who was working in the region of Rezina and just happened to be visiting Balti that evening. I rather boldly told him that he was an answer to our prayers as the Lord had placed on our hearts to visit that part of the country. Pavel invited us back to his village Ciniseuti, and we spent the next days visiting also the surrounding villages where he was planting new churches.

As we spent time with Pavel, we met some of the other church planters in that region. Two different Illies shared with us the struggles and challenges that they faced trying to plant churches in Rezina and Ribnita. In one village we were introduced to Nicu, who we were told was demon possessed, and I was asked as 'the missionary' to pray for his deliverance. We were especially touched and challenged by the great spiritual needs there, and really felt God speaking to us to focus more and seek to help church planting efforts especially in that part of the country.[13]

It was in those summer visits to Moldova in 1996 that I realised just how much I had changed and was changing. Our family's Sunday morning drives to church back in England seemed so distant, as indeed did my old feelings about church and Christians. I had been so embarrassed, even ashamed of telling people about my beliefs growing up, and yet now, here I was full of zeal and passionately taking every opportunity to preach and share about my faith, and even pray for the demon possessed! I mean really – what is that all about? Do these sort of things really happen in the modern age? The book of Acts in the Bible seemed so real – we seemed to almost be reliving parts of it.

We spent that summer travelling from village to village, sharing, singing, preaching, distributing books, eating cherries (and

13 It has been encouraging and exciting to see over the following twenty years how God has brought many people to faith in that area and used also OM to help see churches established and missionaries mobilised and even sent out from there to other countries.

much more), enjoying wonderful fellowship, constantly amazed by the warmth of the reception that we were given by our Christian brothers and sisters. It was our constant prayer that we would not be a burden, but somehow be an encouragement to the believers and a challenge to the non-Christians that we met. After every trip, we arrived home in Austria smelly, (usually having not encountered running water for weeks), exhausted, and yet encouraged and excited at how we had experienced and seen how God had been using us.

Our literature work in Romania continued and we also began to prepare for taking an evangelistic outreach-team to Moldova. Until then, our trips had consisted of me, Helen and a translator (or two). However, in September 1996, we set off again to drive across Hungary. This time we picked up a team of young people that we had recruited in Romania, and we headed back to Moldova to lead an evangelistic outreach-team there for the first time.

We spent just over a week based with a Pentecostal church in Cahul going from schools to kindergartens to factories to market-places, sharing our faith. It was extraordinary how God opened doors and gave wonderful opportunities for us, a group of young people, to share about the hope we have in God and His Son Jesus Christ. In a teacher training college, in the centre of the town, we were told by a rather suspicious school director that we could have just twenty minutes to speak to all the students. Two hundred, sixteen to eighteen year-olds, filed into the large auditorium and not for the first time I wondered, "what on earth are we doing here?", and silently prayed for courage and the right words to speak. We sang, shared and showed a drama describing how our relationship with God is broken but how Jesus came to restore, forgive and offer us a new life. After our twenty minutes we were preparing to finish when the director stood up and addressed us; "Why have we never heard this message before?" she asked us. "Please carry on – tell us more."

Two hours later we were still there, sharing our faith and answering questions that the young people had. Finally, after four hours, we left, having prayed with nine of the students to receive Christ. We introduced one girl, Tania, to a local pastor's wife Mari. When Mari offered to teach Tania English and do Bible studies with her, Tania replied "I'm not so bothered about English but I really want to study the Bible!"

In the evenings we would go to the accommodation blocks at the sixth-form colleges and had opportunities to show Christian films and talk more with the young people. We met Mihai,[14] a young man from a village, who was attending high school in the town of Cahul. Mihai was one of many young people who showed a real interest in meeting foreigners and listening to the message of Hope that we were sharing. After some good discussions we were able to link him up with a local evangelist and they planned to begin studying the Bible together.

One day a brother in the local church suggested that the men from our team go and preach in the local prison. As we handed over our passports and valuables and entered the old, run-down facility we were told that the day before two inmates had been murdered and there was serious tension and unrest amongst the two thousand remaining inmates. As the four of us walked through the small, crowded courtyard I tried not to catch the eyes of the hundreds of men who stared at us. I felt so vulnerable and seriously wondered if we would ever leave that place alive. We were led to a small whitewashed room where a group of eighteen men met us with such joy. We were introduced to this group of men who had all come to faith in the prison. Their clothes were tattered, their raggedy trousers were held up by scraps of string, few wore shoes, and yet the joy in their eyes was so contrasted with the look I had seen in the eyes of the other men in

14 Name changed to protect his identity

the courtyard outside. When these men started to sing I could not believe what I was hearing. Until then, my experience of Russian hymns was that they were slow, monotone and sung with seemingly little feeling or expression. By contrast, as these men stood and began to sing it was almost unbelievable. They all sang at the top of their voices, with eyes closed and the look of joy and peace on their faces was indescribable. There was no doubt that something extraordinary had happened in their lives. They had found something amazing in that prison. Or perhaps *Someone* amazing had found them. The men expressed a love and gratitude in their singing that I had not heard or experienced before. I was reminded of Jesus' words, "I have come to proclaim freedom for the prisoners" (Luke 4:18) and perhaps for the first time in my life I understood those words in a deeper and more profound way. Those prisoners, who were singing with all their hearts, were freer than anyone I had ever met!

Then, there was Serghei, who I met in the market-place.

"Come with me, I want you to meet my friend." The young man was pretty insistent and so ignoring my own safety advice to our team-members, to not go off alone, I followed him through the market-place and into a darkly lit, badly smelling block of flats.

We had been sharing the Gospel to a large crowd of people in Cahul central market and I had watched this young man carefully. There was something about him. He seemed to have a real interest in what we were sharing and as soon as we finished he came over to me. Serghei knew a little English and we tried to talk. He took me to a friend's work-place, in an apartment block, and we spoke briefly about what I was doing in Moldova before I had to return to the team. I gave him some Christian literature and told him that I would pray for him to find the truth. We parted, and whilst he was just one of hundreds of people I met in 1996, I sensed that God was at work in this young man's life, and prayed that somehow we may be able to meet again sometime.

Sometimes people were angry and did not want to listen to the message we shared. Sometimes people were drunk and made disturbances in the various meetings; but the majority of the time we stood before attentive audiences of tens or even hundreds of people, who would listen and were genuinely interested in hearing more about God and His love for them. One lady said to us, "Your words are not like the powerless ones the Orthodox use to preach, but they go to the soul and they touch the heart." I did not feel like a particularly good preacher, and the message we shared was simple, and yet God seemed to be taking our ordinary words and working in people's lives in powerful ways.

In November 1996 we were back in Cahul, again trying to help to mobilise local churches to be active in reaching out to those around them. The journey had been especially eventful. Leaving Austria, this time with two vehicles and a small team of individuals from Europe and North America, who we had recruited for the outreach, we arrived late in Romania, and were already tired before the outreach had even started. We picked up more young people from churches in Romania who joined us; and as we drove across the mountains from Cluj towards Targu-Mures in Romania, the brakes of one of the vans started to fail. The delay set us back further and by the end of the third day, we arrived late at the train station to collect the Ukrainian team-members.

We had missed the train and there was no sign of the Ukrainians! We prayed, and waited, and eventually met them off a later train. It was midnight. There were nine of us, plus our baggage, plus literature and aid packets squashed into our Ford Transit van. Everyone was tired and hungry and we still had a three-hour journey ahead of us to Cahul in the south.

We managed to find a working public phone, change money and buy a small token from someone so that we could make a phone call. The watchman at the Pentecostal Union answered the phone and we were welcomed to sleep on the upstairs floor of the office building. I was disappointed that we would not be in Cahul for the Sunday morning service but we were invited to take part in the service of the new *Filidelfia Church* that was being planted by Doru, a young missionary pastor from Romania, whom we had got to know on our previous visits. The next morning, the worship-time during the service was wonderful. It was unlike anything I had experienced in Eastern Europe before; so genuine and full of life, yet at the same time reverent – and the presence of God seemed so real and tangible. We were truly blessed by the welcome we received in the church and were thankful for the delays we had experienced. As we were leaving a young man called Vasile approached me. He knew some English and shared how he was visiting the church from the north. He had recently been studying in Romania and had come across one of the books OM had printed in Romania: *'The Challenge of Missions'*, by Oswald J. Smith. Vasile shared how this book had impacted his life and how he dreamt of being a missionary and longed to share the Gospel with other people. I had recently been reading through the book of Acts and had seen how the apostle Paul had travelled around as a missionary and taken people along with him on his journeys. So I told Vasile that if he wanted to be a missionary, he should come along with us and join our team. He was a little surprised, especially when I told him that we were leaving in ten minutes so he should hurry!

Vasile had to take care of some business at home, but within a few days he had joined our team, which arrived later that day in Cahul. Again, we stayed in the home of pastor Timofei and were, as always, fed wonderfully – as many chickens, geese and rabbits gave their lives for the missionary cause.

A young lady called Tamara, from a nearby village, was staying with Timofei and his family whilst she studied in Cahul. We invited Tamara to spend time with us as a team. She seemed happy to miss school and travel around to different evangelistic programmes with us. Tamara was as active as everyone else, giving out tracts and inviting people to our different Gospel presentations. We had been using a George Foster tract entitled 'Following Jesus Christ', which we had collected from the printer in Romania earlier on our journey. Tamara seemed very keen to spend time with the strange group of Christian young people and she was very interested in the Gospel message we were sharing. By the end of the week, Tamara approached Helen and said that she also wanted to "follow Jesus Christ". The pastor's wife Jenya got a headscarf for Tamara[15] and she, Helen and the newly converted and covered Tamara, knelt and prayed to receive Christ as Lord and Saviour. We prayed with a number of people as they gave their lives to Christ on that trip, and gave out many Bibles to the new converts, but it was Tamara whom we were particularly excited about. We sensed that God had a special plan for this young lady and were keen to hear and see what He would do in, and through her, in the future.

As we left Moldova and headed back to Austria I felt my eyes had been opened to what God was calling us to do in Moldova in the future. We, of course, were encouraged by the dozens of people who had made a profession of faith. Tamara, amongst others, had come to faith and already was linking with the local youth group and seemed to be active in wanting to share her faith with others. I was especially encouraged to have recruited and mobilised Romanian and Ukrainian young people to join us on the outreach. They all shared about having a life-changing experience as they travelled with us and took part in the mission outreach. Then there was Vasile who had spent the week with us and after the first day had said; "This has been the greatest day of my life! We have preached the Gospel from morning to evening."

15 In many churches in Moldova women are expected to cover their heads when they pray.

The church members we had worked with also seemed to be encouraged by our visit. The leader of one youth group, after a day spent with our team, said to fellow church members, "Why have we never done this before? … Going onto the streets and inviting people to church – we are all called to share the Gospel!" I realised that God was not just calling us to evangelise people in Moldova. We were a part of Operation *Mobilisation*, and to be most effective as missionaries we were not just to try and do the ministry ourselves, but we were to seek to multiply ourselves, to recruit and mobilise others to come along with us and share in the Lord's Great Commission.

Therefore go and make disciples of all nations, baptizing them in the name of the Father and of the Son and of the Holy Spirit, and teaching them to obey everything I have commanded you. (Matthew 28:19–20)

We felt called to help reach people in Moldova with God's love, but our hearts were also burdened for the people of Romania and Ukraine and indeed other peoples in other countries. I began to realise that God could use OM's work in Moldova to mobilise Christians from other countries to come, have a life changing missions experience whilst at the same time helping local believers to reach out to the lost. I also began to see how essential it would be for us to work together, and under the authority of local churches in Moldova, to help them in the mission God was calling them to, rather than us just coming in as foreigners and trying to impose a new way of doing things. I wanted us to work closely with the existing Church, to esteem the Church and to learn together with the Church how to reach the lost most effectively. I realised that our calling as missionaries was to mobilise, equip and help local believers reach out to those who did not know Jesus, rather than just us as foreigners '*do mission*' and then leave.

Our travels to Romania, Ukraine and Moldova continued through 1996 and into 1997 as we spent as much time on the road as we did actually living in Austria. We always tried to include visits to Transnistria on our trips to Moldova and found many of the people to be very open to the Gospel, despite the controls and influence of the very closed authorities. In the village of Molokish Mare we worked with Illie as he planted a church in this small and remote village. We were not allowed into the school or kindergarten to share the Gospel so went out to the fields where everyone was working the land. People gathered around as we set up our sketch board in the middle of the beetroot field and began to sing and share our faith. Everyone seemed very happy to listen and ask questions apart from one very angry lady. She shouted at us and went off to call the police to have us arrested. I was concerned and suggested to Illie that maybe we should leave, but he just laughed and said that the police did not have enough money for fuel to drive from Ribnita, the local town, out to where we were in the fields, so we could just continue. We spent the rest of the afternoon talking and sharing with our new friends in the village and trying to encourage the local believers in their new faith.

It was an exciting way to spend our first years of married life as we drove long distances, talked, shared and dreamt about our future and what God was doing in and through our lives. After one long drive back to Austria in the Spring of 1997, I was particularly tired. Once again we had seen God do wonderful things as He protected, provided and opened doors for us to minister to people together with local churches. However, funny things can happen on a three-day drive home.

Over the previous weeks wherever we had found ourselves in Moldova I had been preaching from a fairly obscure text found in Micah 6:8

He has shown you, O man, what is good. And what does the LORD require of you? To act justly and to love mercy and to walk humbly with your God.

I had sensed God really speaking to me and through me as I preached from this text on a number of occasions, yet, by the time I had driven back to Austria, seeds of doubt had crept into my mind. *"What was I doing? Could I really preach, and were the messages I had shared actually relevant for people? Is this really what God is calling us to do? Is this all really worth it?"*

After the three-day drive I was tired and feeling pretty discouraged.

We arrived back at the office, collected our post and headed home to our apartment in the village of Grossmugl. After showering and deliberating as to whether we should burn or try to wash our clothes, we sat down to look through the letters from home. The first letter I opened was from a wonderful couple from our home church Ashley Baptist. Hedley and Ruth Tipler had always been great encouragers for me. They had given me a 'Christian, student survival pack' when I first headed off to university and prayed, supported, visited and kept in touch with us regularly since we had been on the mission field. Every missionary needs people like the Tiplers for prayer and encouragement. As I read their letter my eyes filled with tears. They wrote of their prayers for us and then at the end of the letter shared a scripture verse which they felt was relevant for us.

He has shown you, O man, what is good. And what does the LORD require of you? To act justly and to love mercy and to walk humbly with your God. (Micah 6:8)

The very same verse that I had felt led to preach from for the previous weeks.

I sat there and realised once again that God was in all of this. I was experiencing too many coincidences for it *not* to be God at work. As I sat in hushed silence I sensed afresh that God Himself was with us. He had called us to this work, He was in control, we could trust Him and we were blessed to have also the support of so many friends, willing to stand with us, believing in us and in the calling God had placed in our lives.

We were already well into the second of our two-year commitment to serve, as a couple, with OM. We felt it was right to lengthen our time on the mission field, and after several days of fasting and seeking God, we felt a deep peace and confirmation that we should commit to working with OM for another two years. But we did not want to stay in Austria. We loved the work in Romania and Ukraine but we were convinced that God Himself was calling us to go and live in Moldova. So, with a sense of God's calling, the affirmation of our OM leaders and the support of our friends and home churches in England, we started making plans for moving into Moldova. Everything was pointing us in that direction – God had confirmed the calling in so many ways. What could possible go wrong?

CHAPTER ELEVEN

Ghandi's Growling

What are you supposed to do when you are sure that you are dying?

The pains in my chest started to come more regularly and became more acute. I looked around the hospital room and was sure that these were my last moments on this earth. So what to do? I took a pen and paper and began writing a letter to Helen. We had been married for just over two years. We had experienced so much blessing and God's provision … but it seemed to be my time to go, so I wrote her a final letter.

I felt that at only twenty-five I was too young to die. There was so much more I wanted to do with my life. I would never be a father, never play football again – and never get to live and serve as a missionary in Moldova. It was this that confused me the most. I knew God was holy and sovereign. I knew He was in control of all things, and that my life was in His hands. To my surprise, I realised that I was not particularly afraid of dying. I knew where I was going – and there was a sense of anticipation – even excitement. But I was sad … for Helen, for my parents – and I was confused about never getting to live in Moldova – but what could I do?

It is at these times that one stops and considers what is really important in life. The words to the song that had so touched me in Guyana, some years earlier, came flooding back to me …

'… if it costs me everything I'll obey …'

During previous years, our vision and passion had been to help mobilise Christians from Romania and Ukraine to reach out to people in Moldova. We had taken the decision to move to Moldova. We wanted, and planned to become real, 'pioneering missionaries,' and do what *real* missionaries do. The plan was to move to a remote community, live amongst the people we sought to reach, evangelise, disciple and plant churches. The adventure was really just about to begin and yet it was now never going to happen. The pains in my chest continued to come in waves – and I was convinced my time was up.

I wrote some more in the letter to Helen, placed the pen down, and lay back in the hospital bed. I closed my eyes and waited. After some time, I opened my eyes and realised that I was still alive, so I decided to write also to my parents. I thanked them for the way they had raised me, for their godly influence in my life, for their discipline and love, and then I lay back down and closed my eyes and waited.

After some time I found that I was still alive and so I also wrote to my friends and shared with them the hope I have in Jesus. I challenged them to consider their own relationship, or lack of, with God. Again, I lay back and waited.

… if it costs me everything …

As the pains increased in my chest I pressed the emergency button and a group of doctors came back into the room. They spoke amongst themselves in hushed voices, and were clearly concerned. The pain in my chest only eased when a doctor sprayed something into my mouth, which I later learnt was nitro-glycerine and was used to improve the circulation of blood to my heart. I was wheeled into an intensive care unit and connected to lots of wires and pipes. That night, as I dipped in and out of consciousness, I kept an eye on the small black screen which reassuringly glowed green and showed that my heart was still beating. Sometime in the middle of the night, the monitor on the other side of me beeped and flat-lined, as the lady in the bed next to me died.

… if it costs me everything …

As medics rushed around her bed, I lay still, waiting and willing my green line to continue pulsing, but slightly morbidly, I was fascinated to see what would happen if it stopped.

———————

It was the summer of 1997. We had been travelling, almost non-stop, to and from Romania, Ukraine and Moldova for two years. That summer we ran the first ever Love Europe campaign in Moldova. It was an incredibly busy time. On the back of lots of driving and tiring trips to Romania and Ukraine, we had recruited two teams of Christians to join us for a summer of evangelism in Moldova. On an earlier trip to Moldova we had lined up churches to work with and we were excited to run the first ever OM 'Love Moldova' Summer Outreach. Attending the Love Europe conference in Hungary, I remembered back to my first experience at such an OM conference in 1992. Had it only been five years ago when I had found myself sitting on a bus heading for Germany – all because I wanted to impress a girl? So much had happened in my life since then. Here I was now, married to the same girl, a 'seasoned' missionary, pioneering a ministry and leading teams into a 'new' country. What a transformation had taken place in my life. God had been at work doing incredible things in me during those five years.

So, in July 1997, we prepared the teams and set out on the two day drive to Moldova. Our two transit vans arrived at the OM Romania base near Brasov late on the first day. I still shudder to remember how close I came to losing eight fingers that evening. We had driven for twelve hours and it was late when we pulled in to the village of Ghimbav. The van behind ours took a corner too tightly, got the chassis caught on a high concrete kerbstone, and could not move forwards or back. We decided to try and ease the van off the concrete slab. As we pushed it started to move, and I got my fingers under the metal lip of the sliding-door, and helped rock the van up and down. Suddenly, the van shifted forward and the chassis lifted off the concrete slab. Having moved a few centimetres, it slammed back down onto the slab with the metal lip of the sliding-door now resting on the slab. I looked down in horror to see where my fingers had been a split second earlier and saw the full weight of the three and a half ton van now resting on the sharp metal rim of the door. It was a sobering experience as I realised how incredibly close I had come to losing my fingers. I do not know how, or why, I moved my fingers away in that final second, and I still shudder to think what would have happened if I had not. As I lay awake that night, praying, the peace of God flooded my heart and I sensed once again God's reassuring hand of protection and blessing upon us. Within a few weeks, I was however, soon to question His working in my life.

We sent one team down to the south to minister with Timofei and his church in Cahul, and Helen and I led a second team to the town of Nisporeni. On a visit to Moldova, a few months earlier, we had been introduced to Victor. Victor was a young evangelist who had trained for a year in the US, and had returned to Moldova to plant churches. He was travelling from Chisinau out to the small town of Nisporeni every week, pastoring a group of ladies who had recently come to faith. Victor's wife Emilia had just given birth to their first child; and spending time with Victor in the spring of 1997, we had been impressed by his hard work, passion and commitment to the Gospel. That summer, we were excited to have an evangelistic team serving with Victor in

Nisporeni, a largely unreached market-town, hidden away in the beautiful Codru forest, in the very heart of Moldova.

The week we spent in Nisporeni was probably the most exciting time that we had yet experienced in Moldova. Our whole team lived in an apartment in a block that had been designated for Transnistrian refugees. We spent the days in the market-place, park, camps and on the streets making friends and sharing the hope we have in Jesus. At that time, we were seeking God about our future and were beginning to feel a call to move to, and live in Moldova full-time. As we shared the Gospel with people that summer, and got to know the sisters in the small church, we sensed a confirmation and conviction that this was the place to which we were called.

Having spent a wonderful week in Nisporeni we spent some days with Sasha, Victor's best friend, who was planting a church in the village of Cojusna. One open-air Gospel meeting was disturbed by a drunk who started attacking us. This man punched the sketch-board so hard, that Helen was using to tell a children's story, that it flew through the air and crashed to the ground. Then he turned towards us. What are you supposed to do when there are a hundred or so people listening attentively to you and an angry, mad-man suddenly comes at you and is about to knock your head off? Just as we were whispering silent prayers to God for protection, a man on a motorbike pulled up. He grabbed the drunken man, planted him on the back of his bike and drove off. I have no idea who this man was. He didn't look like an angel, I was sure that angels would not ride motorbikes without crash-helmets, but whoever he was, God certainly used him to protect us – and allow us to continue to share the Good News.

After Cojusna, we spent the final days of our outreach in a small town called Ialoveni, where we also helped with a new church plant. I had not slept well for weeks and was feeling particularly unwell. Due to the conditions, the mosquitoes, the busyness and pressure of leading the teams, I was feeling increasingly weak and dizzy. It was in Ialoveni that I started to realise that I had a problem – but I didn't realise how serious it was. We finished our time there and began the three-day drive back to Austria. Helen and I had to drive a van each; and after an interminable journey, we finally limped home, with the gearbox broken on one van and the alternator gone on the other. We were exhausted. That evening I could not even stand up in the shower and I went to bed not knowing that I would wake up the next day unable even to walk.

And so it was that I was rushed to a hospital in Vienna, and found myself watching my heart beat on a screen in an intensive care unit.

... if it costs me everything I'll obey ...

I didn't die!

After a few days, I was diagnosed with Acute Rheumatic fever and I spent the next two weeks in hospital. It was explained that some weeks earlier I must have contracted a throat infection, which had not been treated, and the streptococci bacteria from my throat had attacked my heart valves, enlarging my heart to double its normal size. No one knew for certain what this meant for my future, but it was suggested that I would probably either suffer heart problems or rheumatoid arthritis later in life. I was put on a high dose of penicillin, aspirin and many other medicines and was confined to a hospital bed.

After some days, I was taken out of intensive care and placed on the general ward where I shared a room with four other men. 'Ghandi' was in the bed opposite me and spent all day and night growling like dog. It almost certainly wasn't the actual Ghandi from India – but this brown, wizened old man, wrapped in a white sheet, looked like him and kept me awake with his moaning and growling. I felt sorry for him, as I did for another patient who had problems with 'luft'! I had picked up a few German words and phrases along the way, and my stay in an Austrian hospital imprinted some German words forever in my mind. I cannot forget the old fellow sitting on his commode just across from my bed, and the nurses asking him if there had been any 'movement' below. He would look dejected and mournfully cry, 'luft, luft only luft' to the sympathetic looks of the nurses. Those of us in that room with him for two weeks could testify to his serious problems with 'luft', and I do not think I will ever forget the constant sounds of Ghandi growling and 'luft' that filled the room.

On being released from hospital I was told that I must rest for six months. I could not travel during that time at all, and certainly should not consider travelling to Eastern Europe again, as it was considered too dangerous for my heart if I were to catch rheumatic fever again.

I had started to keep a journal a year or so earlier. As I look back through my thoughts, prayers, frustrations, questions and concerns that I recorded at the time, I can see the way the Lord was leading me during those challenging months.

Thursday 20th August, the day I arrived home from hospital, I wrote in my journal …

"In Moldova this summer I felt so close to God as he anointed and empowered me to preach as never before. But now I feel so close to Him [in a different way] as He meets me in a humbled, broken way.

God doesn't want me confidently and busily moving into Moldova. He wants me broken and fearfully and desperately trusting Him as I go. Not in pride of what I can do but in broken humility. King David led the people not with an iron-hand and confidence in his own ability to destroy giants, but in broken humility, after years on the run, having learnt painful lessons whilst hiding in caves. He was only equipped to lead as God wanted when all his pride and confidence in his own abilities had been driven from him and he HAD to trust in God. There was no one or nothing else to trust in, he himself had died to [his] own selfish ambition and pride many years earlier and that is what made him 'a man after God's own heart'"

I can see now, how God was continuing to work in my life, and using the illness to speak about areas of my life that I had not stopped to think about much before.

A few days later, on 23rd August I wrote …

"I thought Isaiah 29:13 was for others – OH NO! It's for me as well. My service isn't enough, He wants all, my life, my brokenness, my humility, my leisure time, a 100% commitment – but as I give it all, Lord help me not to be proud. Yes, you are asking more of me, you're expecting more of me, but only because I'm asking and expecting greater things from you – to do in me and through me great things FOR YOUR GLORY ALONE. Maybe the cost of being a true disciple is far higher than we all realise!"

It was an incredibly difficult and confusing time for us. We remained convinced that God was calling us to move to Moldova. We still wanted to go, but the doctors, our church leaders and the OM leaders were all convinced that this would be too dangerous. We had thought God was in this move to Moldova. We thought He had been calling us, and now, there was so much confusion and concern about my health prospects and our long-term plans.

On the morning of Friday 5th September I wrote …

"THE key issue in our lives is our attitude towards Moldova. We feel it is OUR work, that no one else can do it, we have to be involved, in charge, making decisions. I have taken my responsibility too far – God wants me at a stage where I am willing to give it all up. I am not at that stage yet, Lord please help me!"

That afternoon our OM Field Leader came to visit us in our apartment. Despite my half-hearted protestations, he told us that the outreach we had planned to Moldova in November was to go ahead, but we would not be a part of it. We were not allowed to travel as it was too dangerous for my health. Someone else would be leading the outreach. We had to give up *our* dream, *our* ministry, *our* country – and it was painful.

Over the next days, my journal is full of prayers of repentance as I recognised how proud I had become in my heart.

Then, on September 17th I must have been feeling particularly brave, (or stupid), and I wrote …

"Father, I've had enough. Please change me, humble me – whatever it takes"

Next to this I wrote DANGEROUS in capital letters. (I wonder today if I have the courage to write and really mean such a prayer).

The next day I recorded a sort of conversation with God which I wrote in my journal …

"Father I feel like I'm in trouble – can I ever go and live in Moldova? Deep down I really do trust you, I'm not worried really because I know that the best thing for me will happen. In fact, of course I'm more comfortable to go back home to England, raise a family and be comfortable. The problem is that we plead for workers to be sent to the Harvest Field, so few are willing to go … we are – yes, with some fears, but we are willing to go. SO WHY NOT USE US – SEND US?"

"I am preparing you, breaking you so you trust in me NOT in your own skill and experience.'

"Father will I ever be healed?"

"Do you remember watching the potter spiking the clay to get rid of air-bubbles before making it into a pot?"

Why didn't He ever just give me a straight answer? Why answer my questions with questions? Why was life and faith so complicated? I thought back to a visit to a pottery in Romania, a year or so earlier. I remembered how I had watched with fascination as the potter had worked the clay in order to make it pliable. It had even been spiked to get rid of any air-bubbles before it could be used to make something useful. I realised that I was clay being prepared in the hands of the Master Potter. It was painful but I knew deep down that *the* Potter wanted to make something useful, maybe even beautiful. He was in charge and there is not much the clay can do except just allow the Potter to work.

The next day I read Deuteronomy 31:8, and recorded in my journal …

"The LORD will lead you into the land. He will always be with you and help you, so don't ever be afraid of your enemies."

Written in huge letters below this verse in my journal is the word *HALLELUJAH!* I did not know how or when, but that morning I knew without any doubt that we were going to move to Moldova some time.

Over the next months, I prayed, sometimes cried, and wrote in my journal, as I poured out my heart to the Lord, and tried to understand what was happening to me …

Saturday 20th September

"Thank you Father for my illness,[for] the opportunity to reflect more – to stop and seek you afresh and for your peace which passes all understanding."

Monday 22nd September

"It's not me and God who have been working in Moldova – it is God, all God. He could raise up any one of a billion people to do what I've been doing, it's time to realise this and truly humble myself before the Almighty God."

Thursday 25th September

"Yes our future is uncertain but our God is a rock."

Thursday 9th October

"My will must completely surrender to God."

Friday 10th October

"We are in a battle now, but the fight will be even harder in Moldova. Oh Lord I feel like I cannot handle it. Help me I pray, help us both to trust and put our faith fully in you and draw strength from you."

Over the next months, I received monthly injections of penicillin in my backside which, quite literally took my breath away. It was like being kicked by a horse and I would alternate the side, (learning to turn the other cheek), as the bruising would last for weeks after each injection. I was to continue to receive these injections for the next five years, with Helen learning how to administer the incredibly painful shots – having practised on oranges!

My strength gradually returned. By the end of 1997 we had resumed some of our responsibilities in overseeing the literature ministry in Romania. Our two-year commitment to work with OM was coming to an end, and we spent a few days fasting and seeking God's direction for our future. During that time, we felt an incredible peace and sensed God's clear confirmation for us to move to Moldova – despite the on-going concerns about my health. We returned to England at the end of 1997, needing to talk to our church leaders about this step, aware that many of our supporters were very concerned about us continuing our ministry and travels in Eastern Europe.

On returning to England I spent some time in hospital again. This time British doctors confirmed the original diagnosis and advised me about long-term care. I still, at times, felt some discomfort in my chest, and was often very tired and unable to do any exercise. The advice regarding moving to Moldova was not positive and my journal at that time is full of prayers and realisation that I needed to be patient and trust God to lead us.

On Friday 23rd January 1997 I wrote …

"Today is the day of truth. I will have a final doctor's appointment – our future hangs in the balance. Thank you Father for your peace which surpasses all understanding."

The next day I wrote simply 'Hallelujah!' There was no sign of permanent heart damage. Whilst the doctors were unable to give any guarantees about my long term health, we felt at peace to press on with our plans for moving to Moldova.

Within days, we had received approval from our home church to return to the mission field. We flew to Austria and, collecting our belongings, we drove on to Romania in our trusty, white, Ford Transit van, that now belonged to OM Moldova – the newest field in OM. On Saturday 14th February we arrived with all of our worldly belongings in Brasov, Romania. We planned to be based there for the next months and from there we hoped to launch into Moldova. The plan was for us to travel to Nisporeni, find an apartment and move in.

Six years after I had tried to impress a girl by going on a mission trip, there I was, married to her, driving across Europe, ready to move into a small, remote town in the former Soviet Republic of Moldova. We were about to become *real* missionaries living 'in-country' amongst the people we wanted to reach. We had no idea that within two weeks we would be back in England, and once again seriously questioning our future.

CHAPTER TWELVE

Moving In … Almost

Nisporeni is a small market-town and regional centre of more than forty villages an hour's drive west of the capital Chisinau. During visits there in 1997, God seemed to have confirmed that Nisporeni was to be the place for us to be based.

So it was, that on the 18th February 1998, we were back in Moldova for the first time since my illness six months earlier. We travelled from Chisinau to Nisporeni each day in order to: get more of a feel for the town, try to find an apartment to rent, a guarded placc to park the van and work out what we would need for living there. If in 1995 we had felt like the spies sent out by Moses to check out the Promised Land – to see what it was like; now we felt like the spies heading to Jericho to check out the land – with a view to moving in. We were able to find a two-room apartment right in the centre of the town which had views over the central roundabout, and things seemed to be falling into place for us to make the move.

When Moldova was a part of the Soviet Union, Nisporeni had been a popular tourist location, tucked away in a valley, on the edge of the beautiful Codru forest. Despite the buildings being badly run-down, pot-holed roads, and packs of dogs picking through rubbish and decaying animal carcasses, we fell in love with the small town and its inhabitants. The 'holy' roads did not really matter because you were lucky if you saw one car every five minutes or so. We were fascinated and excited to hear stories of wild boar attacking and eating villagers whilst they collected mushrooms, wolves crossing the river Prut from Romania when it froze, and the struggle to find fresh water. All the water in the centre of the town was polluted with sulphur, which explained the constant smell of rotten eggs in all the houses.

We were going to be living here! … We were going to be living here?

We had visited Nisporeni a couple of times in the previous year, and had got to know members of the Baptist church, as well as Victor, who was planting a Pentecostal church there. In total there were only around twenty evangelical believers in this town of 17 000 people. The surrounding villages were unreached, with no known believers – other than in Vulcanesti, where a small house-church had also begun amongst the Roma population. We were excited at the prospect of helping both churches demonstrate God's love by reaching out to the lost and needy – both in the town and wider region of Nisporeni.

Slavic, the pastor of the small Baptist church, helped negotiate the rent on our apartment. I was frustrated that we had to pay as much fifty lei per month which was equivalent to about eight British pounds. I felt it was too much. We were on a tight budget, but we liked the apartment, had little choice and so agreed to pay. We headed back to Romania excited at the way the Lord had opened doors for us. We slept in the van, in the mountains on the way back to Brasov, and planned to spend a couple of days resting and eating pizza – before packing all our belongings and driving back to Moldova — to our new home.

Within hours of arriving back in Brasov the phone rang. My mother was on the line and she explained that Dad had been taken into hospital with a suspected brain tumour! We had just been with my parents, in England, a few weeks earlier and there had been no sign of any problem. How could this be happening to our family? As we held each other and prayed about what to do, I looked up and saw a poster on the wall of the home where we were staying:

When you pass through the waters,
    I will be with you;
and when you pass through the rivers,
    they will not sweep over you.
When you walk through the fire,
    you will not be burned;
    the flames will not set you ablaze
Isaiah 43:2

As I read these words it was as if God himself was speaking them to me. I sensed that we had some serious struggles ahead, but I also knew that God was going to be with us throughout. We prayed and believed that we should return immediately to be with Mum and Dad. So we drove for twelve hours through the night to Budapest, took a flight to London, and within a day I was standing next to a hospital bed, looking at my father and crying out to God for a miracle.

———————————

My father, Gordon Roger Skirton, was a remarkable man. He had grown up in a small, two-bedroom, council house in Bath, Somerset. The youngest of four brothers and a keen sportsman, instead of pursuing football as a career, like his oldest brother Alan, he had moved to London, obtained a degree in Mathematics, and become a teacher. During his student years, he had started attending a church in Heston, a suburb of London, where he had met Janet – a fashionable and attractive girl from the youth group. They were married in Heston Congregational Church in 1968. The young, newly-married maths teacher, was, over the following years, promoted to head of maths, deputy and later Head Teacher – or Head Master as he preferred. He had a fearsome reputation as a strict disciplinarian.

My childhood memories are happy and safe ones. I remember fondly weekends playing and helping in the garden, family walks, and camping holidays to France in the summer. They are happy, safe and secure memories of growing up in a loving and protected environment. Dad was firm but always fair. Whilst he was secretly introverted, he loved to be the life and soul of parties; telling jokes, cheating at games, and generally having fun, whilst always maintaining a strict discipline – and never, ever publically showing emotion. Dad was an upright and well-respected member of the community and had a strong, if perhaps conservative and traditional, faith in God. I realise that I was never really inclined to rebel because of the love, deep respect and maybe even fear I had of not wanting to disappoint my father.

What do you do when the man who has always been there in your life, the one who is strong and proud, firm but fair, fun-loving yet strict, is lying helpless in a hospital bed – and the prognosis is not good? My journal over the next weeks is filled with prayers and confusion as we did not know whether we should stay in England or continue with our move into Moldova.

On Sunday 1st March I felt God speak so clearly through Psalm 27:14

Wait for the Lord, be strong, take heart and wait for the Lord.

What a great reassurance it was for us as believers to have the hope and certainty that God was in control and my father was in safe hands. Yet, it was still such a difficult time for our family – trying to learn to wait and trust. On Saturday 14th March we received the news that we had dreaded. The results of a biopsy showed that Dad had a brain tumour that was malignant, and the doctors said that he had only months to live!

On the day I turned twenty-six, we decided that we should stay in England, support Mum and nurse Dad, for however long he had left. I wrote that day …

"Lord, this last year Helen and I have been moving constantly. We're not able to settle anywhere. I've had this serious illness and now Dad! It's been the hardest year yet we don't regret a moment of it. In suffering you develop perseverance, character and hope. I love you, I worship you and I rejoice in you. What a great and marvellous God you are!"

Dad knew he was dying. On Thursday 19th March he prayed the simplest, yet most sincere prayer, that I had ever heard him pray: *"Lord we believe in you – we have no doubts!"* From that day he became steadily weaker and weaker. There were occasional days when he seemed to rally, but we all knew deep down that he wasn't going to recover.

I prayed and fasted for miraculous healing. God filled my heart again and again with His peace that surpasses all understanding – but despite my earnest prayers, I sensed that there was not going to be a miracle. I struggled with many questions. Why does God choose to heal some people and not others? Why do good people suffer? If God answers prayers, then why does He not answer our prayers now? Why does He not do what I want Him to do? In the midst of the questions and confusion, there was a constant sense that God was present, that He knew everything, that He was Sovereign and in control – yet there was no Divine intervention and healing. We trusted Him. We knew that He knew best and we experienced His peace – even in the midst of heartbreak.

We struggled to know whether to stay and care for Dad, or continue on with our move to Moldova.

On Thursday 2nd April I wrote …

"I want to go to Moldova soon and yet I am learning patience. I'm reminded that my health is still not perfect, Help me to rest dear Lord when I need to. The man who trusts in his own plans is destined for disaster. The man who trusts in the Lord will see success."

Dad was at home and visited daily by Macmillan nurses who did a wonderful job in helping to keep him comfortable. For two months, I spent hours each day sitting at Dad's bedside. I used the time to continue my theological studies and tried to continue studying Romanian. Even though Dad was rarely able to communicate, it was special for me to be able to spend, what I knew were his last days on this earth, together with him.

On Saturday 25th April 1998, in the early afternoon, my father died.

After lunch I read Psalm 46, Psalm 121 and part of Psalm 27 to him. As I read about the Lord being with us, a beautiful sense of acceptance and reassurance flooded the room and Dad seemed to relax. His breathing became slower and slower – as I read from Romans 8 I knew he was leaving.

I am sure that nothing can separate us from God's love – not life or death …

Nothing in all creation can separate us from God's love for us in Christ Jesus our Lord!

Mum and Adam came into the room, Dad took one more breath and he was gone.

I will always be thankful to God for the way both of my parents raised me and the values they installed in me as a child. So often I am reminded of my father. When I look in the mirror I see him, when I discipline my children, when I chair meetings and even when I laugh, I hear him. When I socialise and push myself to be more extroverted, and have fun and cheat when playing games with my children, I so often am reminded of him and his influence in my life. I see how his discipline, and values continue to influence who I am and how I live – I am however trying to learn that I do not have to suppress my emotions and feelings all the time!

Helen and I spent the following days with Mum and Adam preparing for the funeral. But, life went on, and we felt that our calling to Moldova was as strong as ever. So within a few weeks, we had flown back to Budapest, picked up the van, and once again headed east to Romania.

On 19th May 1998 we finally drove across the mountains and moved into Moldova – expecting to be there for maybe a couple of years. We had no idea that seventeen years later we would still be here!

CHAPTER THIRTEEN

I Need Meat!

Bang, bang, bang! Silence!

Bang, bang, bang. Then followed angry shouting and more banging. Someone had climbed the communal staircase of our apartment block and was trying to get in through our front door. They sounded desperate. They sounded angry – and they were not giving up!

It was our first night in Nisporeni and we had been woken by the banging. There was no electricity, and as I huddled in the darkness next to Helen, on the mattress, on the floor of our living room, I wondered what I should do. I turned my torch on and looked around for some sort of weapon to defend us. A metal bucket? A wooden chair maybe? I had no idea what I could use.

Bang, bang, bang! I am sure I was just as scared as Helen, but I tried not to show it. What could I do? We were on the fourth floor – there was no escape through the windows. It was after midnight, and the silence and darkness were being broken only by this frantic crashing and angry shouting, as someone tried to get in. How long would the door hold out?

We huddled together and prayed. Within minutes the banging stopped and whoever it was had left. I would like to say that we were flooded with a 'peace that surpasses understanding', but the reality was that the fear took a lot longer to go away. We lay awake. We were scared!

Earlier that evening we had opened a tin of Quality Street chocolates – left over from Christmas, and carefully packed and transported across Europe. The apartment had no furniture, and so we sat crossed-legged on the floor, with boxes of our possessions scattered around the room. Our bed was a mattress on the floor, and as we shared out the chocolates I tried to smile reassuringly at Helen – but silently I was asking myself, "What have we done?" Helen looked at me and could not hold back the tears any longer – and started crying. Six years after my first missions experience in Estonia, trying to impress a girl; and now here I was, sitting on the floor opposite her – my wife – in some remote corner of Europe, hidden away in a small town, in a rundown apartment, with no electricity, gas or running water, in what felt, quite literally, like the middle of nowhere. Whatever was I thinking?

We had driven into Chisinau two days earlier, on 19th May 1998. It was late in the evening and the drive from the border had been the longest and darkest imaginable. The fog that evening was so thick that we could not see more than a few yards along the road and so driving was slow. As we drove down Stefan Cel Mare, the main street, everything was deserted. No traffic. No people. Just a thick, dark fog – we had come to live here?!? I again heard a mocking, sneering voice telling me how stupid I was to want to come and live in this dark, unwelcoming place. I drove silently, knowing Helen was thinking the same as me – but not knowing what I could possibly say to encourage her.

And then I saw it – a sign of God's blessing, a sign of hope, a sign that filled my heart with joy and reassurance. For out of the dark fog, I saw first of all dim, and then getting brighter and brighter, golden arches that indicated blessing, warmth, hope, prosperity and cheeseburgers. Yes – it had happened! Since our previous visit to Moldova, McDonalds had opened a restaurant on the high street! It may sound like the most ridiculous thing now, but at the time, even if God Himself had painted a rainbow across the sky, I am not sure it would have brought as much reassurance and joy into our hearts, as seeing that restaurant on such a dark, unwelcoming night. Whatever our living conditions were going to be like, whatever we would have to eat over the next months, I knew there was one familiar place, selling artificial and unhealthy food, that we would be able to escape to now and again.

After one night in Chisinau we drove with Victor out to Nisporeni. He helped carry all of our things up to our apartment and arranged a guarded parking-space for the van.[16] Then he said goodbye and we were on our own. For the next six months Victor came every Thursday and Sunday to lead the church services, but between these visits, Helen and I were on our own. We had learnt a few phrases of Romanian/Moldovan, but we could barely communicate to people, and there we were in what felt like an incredibly remote place, very much on our own yet so aware that we were not alone.

We survived our first night in Nisporeni, and for the next two-and-a-half years, no-one ever tried to break down our door again. It just happened on that first night, that, probably a drunken man had mistaken our apartment for his, and angrily tried to get in. We knew that our battle was not against flesh and blood but against principalities and powers. This was real. We really felt that we were living in enemy territory. I would like to sound spiritual and say that we knew God was with us and so we felt no fear. Of course we knew He *was* with us, but at times it was scary in those early days, living on our own in our little apartment. We

16 It was very dangerous to leave vehicles unattended at night so we always had to find someone to allow us to park our van in their courtyard.

tried to be courageous, but I came to understand that greatest courage is found not in the absence of fear but when fear is greatest. We learnt to press on – trusting and knowing that God held us safely in His hands.

After a few days, we would again hear knocks on our door, but every time we opened the door, we heard scurrying and saw children disappearing quickly down the stairs. After some tries, we managed to open the door and 'catch' four girls running up and down our stairs. They were too afraid to stay at the door, but they were intrigued to try and get to know these strange foreigners who had come to live in their town. Ira, Natasha, Natasha and Ana sometimes would come along to the church services on Sunday, and so we knew them a little. Soon, they started coming to our apartment every day after school. We welcomed them, and they were able to help us begin to learn Moldovan and practise the words and phrases that we were trying to learn from our books.

Our days consisted of prayer and Bible study in the mornings, trying to write emails and connect to the outside world by dial-up modem,[17] language studies and conversation practice with the girls in the afternoons, preparing sermons for Thursday and Sunday church services and fetching water.

I had never realised how important water was until I lived in Nisporeni. In order to have fresh water we had to walk fifteen minutes up a hill to a spring, fill canisters and then walk back to our apartment and up four floors. Twice-a-day I would make this journey and my muscles strengthened as I carried 30–40 litres[18] of water back from the spring a couple of times each day. During the summer it took even longer, as the spring would dry up almost to a trickle, and it was not unusual to be pushed out of

17 At a speed of 468 bits per second our connection was more than twenty thousand times slower than our present 10 MB broadband connections
18 6.6–8.8 gallons or 7.9–10.5 gallons in US

the way by a big cow as we tried to collect water. It was however in the winter, when temperatures dropped to $-30\,C$ $(-22\,F)$, that it became even more challenging. We would use the water for cooking and washing, before it went into a bucket for washing clothes before finally making it into the bucket that was used for flushing the toilet.

Water quickly became our most precious commodity. We boiled the water for at least ten minutes, using a cooker connected to a gas bottle, before letting it cool and using it for drinking or cooking. Electricity was rationed, and we would have it for a couple of hours each morning, and sometimes in the evenings. So we would charge up our lanterns during those hours, and get the apartment ready with candles for night time. When it was dark, it was really dark. Not a light could be seen for miles in any direction when the electricity was off, and we became used to the eerie silence that accompanied these true blackouts each night. We got used to reading by candlelight and going to bed early. There was nothing else to do – and it was the best way of keeping warm!

The winters were harsh, and with no heating in our block, we used electric heaters when the electricity was on, and sat huddled in the kitchen with the gas bottle cooker giving out some heat, at other times. Our neighbours below sometimes had a wood-fire burning in their apartment and so we were lucky that some heat would emanate from their apartment into our bedroom – but our living room remained icy-cold, and we rarely used it in the winter.

After a couple of weeks, the fiercely rationed tin of Quality Street chocolates had been used up, as had most of the other treats we had brought with us from England. We were able to buy fresh bread each day and to my 'joy' cabbage was available in abundance – as were yoghurts. But our diet was very limited – and I started to long for meat. Finally, I persuaded Helen to pluck up courage, and so she braved the market on her own, and with her limited Moldovan approached a man who had half a pig lying on a piece of newspaper on the ground. She boldly approached and pointing at the pig said the words she had been practising for days, "vreau porc va rog" (I want pork meat please). The man looked at her and started asking questions to which Helen nodded nervously. He motioned for her to step back, and a large meat cleaver was wielded above his head. Down it came, Helen paid the man and with blood spattered shoes she hurried home with her treasure wrapped in newspaper. That night we had meat to go with our bread, cabbage and yoghurt!

On 3rd June 1998 I recorded in my journal …

"It is both wonderful and strange to finally be here in Moldova after three and a half years of praying and preparing. We feel excited, yet a little afraid. Alone, yet making lots of new friends. Bold when sharing our faith, yet humbled when we see the faith of others. Overwhelmed by the physical and spiritual needs, yet secure in the knowledge that God is big enough to meet them all. Small, weak and insignificant, yet knowing that He has called us here and we can do all things through Christ who gives us strength."

My diary was filled over the next months with entries that speak of broken telephones, mice, pains in my ears, jaw, back and chest, prayers that I would not become seriously ill again and regular updates about stomach problems due to water and food issues. Every month, is also noted "Injection right/left" as Helen kept attacking me with needles and I continued to alternate the punishment – and turn the other cheek!

We had brought small vials of penicillin with us from England, and Helen would make up the solution whilst I prepared myself for my monthly torture. As it became hot in the summer, we had problems with the solution crystallising too quickly, and Helen not being able to pump it into me. There was nothing for it but to brave the local hospital and ask for assistance.

We had visited friends in the hospital a couple of times, and also gone with the young people from the church to share the Gospel with people there. I was always shocked to see the conditions and had spent the year silently praying that I would never have to enter a Moldovan hospital as a patient. As I lay on my stomach on an old hospital bed I realised that God had not answered *that* prayer.

We explained our need for a thicker needle and I lay with my backside bared as a variety of nurses stood around and discussed my case. We were the only foreigners in the town; most people had never met a westerner before, (or it seems, seen a western bottom – which seemed to be quite an attraction), and the nurses were keen to make a good impression. A couple of them had a try with our needle and failed; so they called for reinforcements. As other nurses filled the room, I lay with my bottom bared to the world, and silently asked God why He had called me to this place. The group of nurses retreated to a corner of the room discussing my case; and then I glimpsed the largest, scariest nurse I had ever seen. She walked into the room, the other nurses parted like the Red Sea as she strode purposefully forward, obviously scorning the inability of the other nurses to administer a simple injection. If someone had told me that this nurse had represented the Soviet Union in shot put at the 1980 Moscow Olympics I would not have been surprised. She rolled up her sleeves, and to my horror, very deliberately took out a syringe the like of which I had never seen in my life. From where I was lying the needle looked to be the size of a pencil, and the syringe the size of a Coca-Cola can. Surely this sort of needle was only used on horses – but before I could say anything, she had strode across the room, on a mission, physically pushing other nurses out of the way, and I closed my eyes and tried not to scream. She had no problem getting the penicillin into me. As I hobbled back to our apartment I realised I had been wrong – she wasn't a shot putter – her sport must have been the javelin!

CHAPTER FOURTEEN

God at Work

For the second time in my life I thought I was dying.

It was 20th February 1999. We had not been eating well. The town's supply of fresh vegetables, fruits and bizarrely yoghurts, had finished some months earlier. As a flu virus swept through the town, the hospital began to fill up, and we heard daily on the radio of the rising death-toll.

We had experienced flu before in England, but had never felt like this. With no heat, limited electricity and thick ice coating the inside of our windows, we huddled together in bed, trying to keep warm, barely able to get to the bathroom, let alone fetch water from the spring. We were miserable. More than twenty people died in the town that week and there were times when we wondered if we would add to that number. However, by God's grace, after five days in bed, we were able to return to normal life – although my aches and pains continued and Helen could not shake off a cough for weeks afterwards.

That summer a dysentery epidemic also swept through the town, again killing more than twenty people. We, along with everyone in our block, were visited by health-inspectors who were trying to pinpoint the source of the epidemic. They wanted to know if we had been affected by the disease. I tried to explain, in my broken Moldovan, that we had had upset stomachs every week for the past year and would probably not know if we had dysentery or not. As it was, we survived these struggles and pressed on in the ministry that God had called us to – but we did feel that we needed to take better care of ourselves.

Realising that we needed to eat more healthily we started shopping more often in Chisinau. Western style supermarkets were beginning to open and vegetables and fruit could now be bought all year round. We also became more familiarised with the McDonalds menu, which we knew was unhealthy, but at least there was no cabbage in the burgers!

Sister Nina, an old Russian babushka, who had moved to Nisporeni from Kazakhastan and come to faith, seemed to believe that it was her personal mission in life to look after and provide health advice for the 'foreign missionaries'. Grated potatoes were brought around when Helen had a cold;[19] and when Nina discovered that Helen had an upset stomach, she arrived at our door with a mysterious bundle of newspaper. Carefully unwrapping her precious bundle, Nina produced dried pieces of chicken stomach which she insisted would make a wonderful soup – and heal Helen's stomach problems. When challenged about how effective this would prove, Nina asked indignantly in Russian if we had ever seen a chicken be sick? We admitted that we had not and she triumphantly exclaimed that this was due to their strong stomachs and hence the soup!

One autumn morning, as we sat huddled in our small kitchen trying to keep warm, Helen suddenly said that she would love some broccoli. Years of cabbage had taken their toll also on her and out of the blue she suddenly had a craving for a fresh, green, healthy head of broccoli. We had never seen broccoli in Moldova,

19 To be placed on her chest as a compress to draw out the virus.

(not even the new supermarket in Chisinau had such 'exotic' vegetables), and so we knew that Helen's dream of broccoli would remain just that, a dream. That afternoon, as we prepared our cabbage and potatoes for dinner, there was a knock at the door. Nina was there smiling away with her only two teeth protruding over her upper lip. She explained that she had just been attending her allotment and something strange was growing there. She removed from her bag a huge head of … *broccoli,* and asked us if we knew what it was! Nina said that she had received a packet of mixed vegetable seeds as humanitarian aid the previous spring, and had planted them, only to find that a whole bunch of strange new plants had appeared, and she didn't know what to do with them. I was tempted to tell her that the broccoli was highly toxic and offer to dispose of it for her. Helen however, more generously, explained that broccoli was very healthy and she should boil and eat it. Nina thrust the broccoli into Helen's hands explaining that she would not trust feeding such strange, new plants even to her chickens. And so, that evening we ate broccoli, and sensed God's smile as we marvelled at His incredible grace and provision.

As I read through my journal from those years, I see that, despite the occasional miraculous provision of green vegetables, we were constantly struggling with all sorts of minor illnesses, and that it was a particularly testing time for us. Helen would often walk to the three pharmacies in town, trying to find medicines that our *'Where there is no Doctor'* book would recommend for me. It seemed as if all the medicines I had taken during my spell of rheumatic fever a few years earlier, had weakened my immune system considerably, and I was constantly fighting something.

Sister Galea was a young doctor from the local hospital and a member of the Pentecostal church. She would often advise us on medicines available in Nisporeni. One night, when I had a reoccurrence of a throat infection, which was considered particularly dangerous due to my previous illness, Galea strongly advised that

I receive an intravenous drip. Afraid of the hospital, (the conditions as well as the nurses), and still sore from the 'javelin in bottom' experience, Galea agreed to come to our apartment and administer the drip. I lay in bed feeling sorry for myself as she tried to get the needle to stay in my arm at the right angle. In the end Galea sat for hours, through the night, holding the needle in place, and ensuring I received the medicine. It was this sort of sacrificial love that the handful of believers in Nisporeni often showed to us, which so encouraged us and helped us to press on – despite the challenges that we faced.

So much could be written about our adventures in those early months. The monthly walk to the gas bottle station carrying our 40kg (88lbs) bottle was always challenging, as was the two of us trying to carry a three-piece suite and double-bed up eight flights of stairs on our own. It was not an easy time at all, and my journal in those early years is filled with prayers for safety and healing for our weak, western bodies.

But, the conditions, however challenging, were not going to stop us. We were in Moldova, doing what we had dreamed of doing for years. We had also made friends at the local Baptist church, and they changed the time of their church services so that we could attend their mid-week meetings as well as those at the Pentecostal church. Each week I would preach twice at the Pentecostal church, once or twice at the Baptist church and usually twice at village church plants. Helen was leading a discipleship group for the young girls who were still visiting our apartment, and she also helped run the Sunday schools in Nisporeni and the surrounding villages. It was the most wonderful time as we befriended people, learnt the language, and lived with and amongst the people we loved and longed to reach out to more and more.

By the summer of 1999 we had been married for nearly four years, and we hoped to start a family. The sisters in the churches were concerned that we did not yet have children and had been talking to Helen, offering advice, and assuring her of their prayers. Some of the advice amused us, but also touched us, as we learnt about our friends' love and concern for us as a couple.

One day, I had a meeting in Chisinau, and drove the hour on my own through the forest. We were no longer so concerned about bandits stopping the car, as we were about wild pigs on the road or cowboy hatted policemen stopping us. It was no real shock when I was stopped on a remote stretch of the main road, in the heart of the forest, but the conversation that followed, in Moldovan, was for me bizarre and I attempt to recreate it below …

Suspicious policeman motioning to me menacingly; *"Papers!"*

I hand over my car papers

Surprised policeman; *"You are a foreigner – what are you doing here?"*

"I am a Christian missionary, I work with churches, I help churches." (In fairly simple Moldovan)

Increasingly interested policeman; *"You are a foreigner, you speak our language! Are you here alone?"*

"No, I am here with my wife."

"Is she Moldovan?"

"No, she is English like me."

"So, you are a foreigner, living here in Moldova with your English wife – how long have you been married?"

"About four years" – starting to feel more at ease with the friendly policeman.

"So how many children do you have?"

"None"

Awkward silence – *"Oh – I am so sorry. Do you want children?"*

"Well yes …"

"Look, I have an uncle who works in a hospital in Chisinau. I could arrange for you to have some tests and get some advice if you like."

149

Had I just hear him correctly? Here in the middle of the forest, a policeman has stopped me and is giving me family planning advice!

I never visited the policeman's uncle, but within weeks we were thrilled to discover that Helen was expecting. We started making plans and discussing where we would give birth, but not long after that Helen became poorly and suffered a miscarriage. It was Wednesday 29th September 1999 and Helen spent the next days visiting the hospital, and recovering in bed. Until that time, our married life had consisted more often of me being the sick one whilst Helen remained strong and healthy. Now, it was my turn to try and care for and encourage Helen – and it was not an easy time. A couple of weeks later we were flying back to England for my grandmother's funeral.

It was in times like these that I would turn to the Apostle Paul's encouragement to the Christians in Philippi. I had often read the letter to the Philippians, but it had been on an earlier journey through Eastern Europe that God had really spoken to me clearly from the text

Rejoice in the Lord always, I will say it again rejoice. (Philippians 4:4)

We were on our way to Moldova. Having left Austria early in the morning, it was only the first day, somewhere in the middle of Hungary, when the wheel of the van suddenly made a horrendous noise and I pulled over to the side of the road as quickly as I could. I am not a mechanic, but I knew that we had a serious problem. We managed to limp into a side road where there were some agricultural buildings. We parked, and tried to decide what to do.

These were, of course, in the days before we had a mobile phone. Our grasp of Hungarian was limited only to ordering food in McDonalds, so there we sat in the middle of a strange country, alone, frustrated, and with few options.

We prayed, and within minutes a man came along who seemed willing to help us. Through gestures, funny noises, and probably telling him that we had a cheeseburger in our wheel, we sort of made ourselves understood. He left, and within an hour was back with a man whom we assumed was a mechanic. The man took the wheel off, motioned that he knew what the problem was, wrote down an amount of money and looked at us. I nodded, and he was gone – maybe to buy us a cheeseburger, maybe to buy a part for the wheel, we really could not be sure.

I was frustrated. No, actually I was impatient and angry. I had a plan, a schedule to keep. I needed to be in Romania that evening. I had lined up lots of meetings across the country over the next few days, before we were due to arrive in Moldova a week or so later. This delay was going to put all my plans out of sync. and I was fed up. I picked up my Bible and sitting on a chunk of concrete next to our van, opened randomly to Philippians chapter four. I had read this text many times before, but it was as if I read it for the first time that day.

Rejoice in the Lord always!

Rejoice – ha!!! You have got to be kidding me! I am sitting in a forgotten corner of a very foreign country without so much as a cheeseburger. I am wasting time and all my carefully laid plans have gone out of the window because of this stupid van and stupid wheel and stupid everything! If the *'great'* apostle Paul were here experiencing this frustration with me, then he would not be so quick to write such super-spiritual rubbish about 'rejoicing always' – that just is not always possible – life happens and things go wrong and we just cannot rejoice all the time!

And then I heard that familiar, loving, yet firm Voice. Once again it was not audible, but as clear as anything I heard a simple question: *"Where was Paul when he wrote this letter?"* … And I repented!

I remembered that Paul had written those words whilst suffering in prison, and I realised in a deeper way just what he was meaning. I truly did ask God for forgiveness that day, realising that going through life complaining just doesn't help anyone. As a Christian I *can* rejoice in all circumstances, whatever happens, whatever I face in life, because He is always there, He is always comforting. Even if I don't always feel His presence, I know that one day all I see here on earth will be gone – and I have the promise and assurance of eternity with Him. I could rejoice then and I still can today! Even if my car breaks down; even if I become ill; even if my wife loses our baby – He is sovereign. He loves us, and knows what is best for us and we can worship Him and rejoice in Him always.

Within a couple of hours the man had returned. A wheel bearing was replaced and we were on our way. I thanked God for the lesson that day, that even, and especially in frustration and suffering, we can draw closer to Him and continue to rejoice always.

Whenever we faced trials or struggles, we always sensed God working in us and giving us His grace and strength to press on – and even to rejoice. On Monday 12th October 1999 we were back in Moldova and I wrote …

"Thank you Lord for calling us here! What a privilege to know you and serve you. Thank you that even after feeling a little down in the last days, you have refreshed and encouraged me. You've reminded me that I'm here because of YOUR calling not because of my plans, because you love and value people here. Help me to show and demonstrate your love. Help me to value people ahead of my plans."

During 1998 and 1999 we saw God working in amazing ways. Dozens of people committed their lives to Jesus and joined one of the small evangelical churches that we were helping to plant.

Some of these people fell away – often due to persecution from friends and family members and sometimes due to alcoholism. However, we saw God opening people's hearts and there was a wonderful hunger for God's Truth. Evening services were especially well-attended in the winter when there was no electricity. The church rooms were well-heated with wood stoves, candles provided light and there was little else for people to do in the town.

I preached regularly in both churches series on: the parables, basic Christianity, an overview of the Bible and many other subjects. I was not calling for people to change their religion but for people to come to a personal faith in God through His Son Jesus. Both Helen and I had serious stomach upsets most weeks which made the long walk to get water for the toilet very difficult at times. I was always intrigued to see that often before preaching engagements at significant outreach services I would usually get an upset stomach. So many of my sermons in those years were preached, (with Victor translating), having spent the previous night running to the toilet, and many mornings I was sorely tempted to call in sick. Often I would find myself walking up the hill to the church building, wondering how I would make it through the service, let alone preach a message. I saw the reality of the apostle Paul's words: *"When I am weak then He is strong"* (2 Corinthians 12:10). I must be a very slow learner because He still allows me to be weak so very often!

There were thirty, or so people, now attending services at the Pentecostal church and about the same number at the Baptist church. That first summer there was a joint baptism service held beside the local lake and a further fifteen believers were baptised.

Being a market town, people from surrounding villages would come to Nisporeni on a Sunday to buy and sell produce and animals. It was fairly common to see sacks containing pigs or goats under the church benches during church services; but one Sunday morning, when some chickens escaped from a sack in the middle of my sermon, Victor had to stop the service and announce that people should not bring animals to church!

We were excited to see all that God was doing in Nisporeni, yet we longed for the fifty-thousand people from surrounding communities to also have the opportunity to hear the Gospel. As we prayed for the region and villages too, God began to open doors for the Gospel in amazing ways. As people from the villages visited Nisporeni, so we would get invitations to go and hold Gospel meetings in their homes. Individuals and families from Vanator, Guareni, Maranici, Soltanesti, Cioresti, Vulcanesti and Micleuseni all came to faith and invited us to preach in their villages also. We quickly came to see that the harvest was truly plentiful, but the workers were few. Some wonderful things were happening but we needed more people to work with us.

We mobilised young people from both churches, (who were beginning to come to faith), to travel with us to the different villages. Each village was different and it was fascinating to see how God seemed to open the hearts of some people to receive the Good News whilst others became angry and even violently opposed us and the message we were trying to share. New believers in Marinici were beaten by neighbours. Christians in Vanator were threatened and their small church building was completely destroyed with other villagers stealing the roof, bricks and leaving nothing but the foundation. In Cioresti, our van was attacked and the windscreen smashed as we shared the Gospel in the local culture house (village hall). It was, however, in the village of Micleuseni, that we faced some of the biggest challenges, (threats and our van tyres deflated or punctured), but we also experienced the biggest breakthroughs and saw the most fruit from our work.

In my journal on Thursday 15th October 1999, I wrote …

"The battle is raging! The god of this age has blinded so many people here, especially in the villages. Yesterday windscreen smashed,

and I hear that the government is passing a new law to make pros-
elytising illegal. Lord please work in Moldova – keep the door open
I pray!"

Costea, from Micleuseni, had turned up at the Pentecostal
church meeting in Nisporeni one Sunday. He had been working
in Moscow and having met some Christians there, had decided to
follow Christ. On returning to Moldova, he had found the local
church in Nisporeni, fifteen kilometres from his village, and was
excited to meet other believers.

Costea invited Victor to begin church meetings in his home in
Micleuseni, and so in 1998, just as we arrived in Nisporeni, a new
church plant also began in Micleuseni. Costea faced great oppo-
sition from family and friends, but remained faithful to his new
faith, and opened his home for church meetings every Sunday.
After the morning services in Nisporeni, the youth group would
squash into our van and we would travel with Victor to Micleuseni, where we preached, shared, sang and evangelised.

Over the months, we saw Costea's family come to faith, and
then neighbours and friends also started to attend the church services. Helen led Sunday school meetings for more than a dozen
children, Victor and I preached, taught and answered questions,
and we saw how the Lord added weekly to the number who were
being saved.

One Sunday afternoon, as I preached, an older lady who had
never attended the meetings sat at the front of the small room
crying. She wept all through the service, and as we closed she
came forward and shared her story. Cristina was sixty-seven years
old and had grown up in a family of Baptist believers. During
communist times she saw the persecution and deportation of
Christians to Siberia and had rejected the faith of her parents.
She married a non-believer, against her parents' advice, and spent
the next forty years living away from God. Cristina shared how
she always knew the truth in her heart, but that she had turned

her back on her faith for so many years. Her husband had not permitted her to attend Evangelical church services, and so she had, for nearly half a century, drifted away from the Lord.

Cristina explained to us that her tears on that Sunday morning were tears of joy. Her husband had died a few months earlier and she said that she had prayed and asked God to give her a new life, and forgive her for her sins. When she heard of the new Gospel meetings taking place in her village she had attended, with some scepticism, but shared with us that the memories of her childhood church services had come flooding back as she had heard the singing and listened to our words. That Sunday afternoon, Cristina knelt, prayed and cried out to the Lord in repentance with an incredible sincerity – as she received Jesus as her Lord and Saviour. She later shared with us how her family and friends tried to turn her back away from this 'new faith' but she said she had returned to the Truth and would never turn her back on Jesus again.

Cristina was one of the first believers in Micleuseni to be baptised, and within two years there were around fifteen members of the church with up to fifty attending the weekly meetings and a couple of dozen children regularly attending Sunday school.

As we ministered in Nisporeni, we remained in contact with the outside OM world via our dial-up internet connection. We wrote prayer requests, ministry reports, and tried to encourage other OM offices to recruit people to join us in the Harvest that was taking place in Moldova. Marianne from Switzerland joined us, as did Julia from America, and Mirela and Corinna from Romania made our team truly international.

That autumn we received a humanitarian aid transport. It arrived in an Austrian registered truck, driven by a Finn, containing clothes and shoes from Switzerland and food from Finland, packed by a Japanese lady, and with finances raised by an American missionary living in the Czech Republic. The whole world seemed to be hearing about, praying for and helping OM's ministry in little Moldova to take off!

At the same time it was an incredibly steep learning curve for me. I had to learn to communicate cross-culturally and not just think about and lead myself and Helen, but also care for and lead a team of very diverse people involved in a fast-growing ministry.

On Monday 23rd November 1999 I wrote …

"The hardest week ever! Mirela left, Corina is ill, misunderstanding with Baptist church, my relationship with 'J' on the line, van broken down, snowed in, no electricity, very cold, still tired after outreach. DESPERATE! Ill and on antibiotics, nauseous and dizzy. Yet your grace is sufficient – just about! Lord help resolve these problems but above all please resolve the [bad] attitudes in my heart."

Saturday 28th November

"Who would [choose to] be a Christian leader

I ask for your refining fire in my heart dear Lord. Even if that means hardships and struggles.

What use is it for a man if he gains the whole world yet loses his soul?"

Monday 30th November

"After the last difficult weeks, God really met me and spoke more to my heart about serving Him [in] love and humility. Thank you Lord for blessing and strengthening me so much.

Now I feel tired and have headaches and more pains in my chest than usual. Help me to trust you Lord and to be strong!

"He is no fool who gives what he cannot keep, to gain what he cannot lose" – Jim Elliot [20]

In the midst of the challenges, difficult living conditions and language learning, we saw God working in wonderful ways during those years. In the summers of 1999 and 2000 we were able to

20 Jim Elliot was one of five missionaries killed while participating in Operation Auca, an attempt to evangelise the Huaorani people of Ecuador in 1955.

mobilise both the evangelical churches in Nisporeni to organise kids and youth camps. Hundreds of children and young people took part in fun activities as well as having the Gospel clearly presented to them. Many made professions of faith during that time, and the youth groups in the churches grew through these summer events.

As we were the only foreigners in the town sometimes people would come to our door and ask for help. One morning, a little girl Lillia, who sometimes came to the church, brought her brother with her and asked if we could give them some money for sweets. Lillia explained that it was Victor's birthday, he had not received a present and that they had no money. Helen asked Victor how old he was and he very proudly said "six-and-a-half". The two children exchanged guilty glances when they realised their mistake and Helen pointed out that it wasn't his birthday. Lillia then explained that it was one year since Victor was five and a half and so it was his birthday. We ended up giving them some sweets for his 'birthday'!

Those years in Nisporeni were life-changing for us as well as for many people we befriended. We were always trying to learn the language better and saw steady progress, although it was not always easy trying to communicate. After just over a year of living in Moldova, and struggling with the language, I found myself one Thursday evening in the village of Vanator for our weekly service. However, for the first time there was no one there who could translate my sermon. And so it was that in Sister Maria's front yard, under the grape vine, I stood up in front of ten or so people, and attempted my first sermon without translation. The believers and visitors that day were very kind and encouraged me as I stumbled through the message, but it was with a sense of relief that I came to the end. However, for me it was a significant step. After a year of living in Moldova I was able to preach in Moldovan, all be it haltingly, with many mistakes and with a horrendous accent.

And so it was that we spent two-and-a-half years living in Nisporeni. Helen was constantly by my side, shopping, cooking, counselling, ministering, visiting people, helping fetch water and administering those bruising, monthly injections. By the summer of 1999, we had mobilised groups of young people from the churches to go through the whole town, speaking to people and sharing their faith. One elderly man, sitting at his gate, greeted us and welcomed us to sit and talk. We spoke to him about the hope we have in Christ and explained that our religion should not just be a series of traditions and rules that we try to follow to get to a God who is distant. We shared that God has come to us, and that we can truly experience a relationship with this living and loving God, through His Son Jesus Christ. The man stopped us and said, *"I like what you are saying, because I know they are not just words. I have seen what you people are like who attend that church on the hill. Your faith is real to you, you really demonstrate the Truth by living out what you say. I have heard how you Christians do not just speak words, but really help each other and demonstrate God's love. For you, Christian faith is not just words but actions."*

I was so encouraged to hear this from someone who, as far as I knew, had never attended an evangelical church. He had not just heard some words, but had seen a difference in the lives of those who were attending the churches we were trying to help. It was so encouraging, God had been working in and through us, yet we were beginning to feel that it was time for us to move on.

By the end of 2000, our team had grown and now consisted of me and Helen, a Romanian couple, two Moldovans and German, Swiss and American ladies. We were encouraged at the way we had been able to help the two churches in Nisporeni and in the handful of village church plants. However, we sensed that God was calling us, as OM, to become more involved in the whole country, rather than just one region.

And so, after two-and-a-half years of living in Nisporeni, Helen and I felt that God was calling us to develop further OM's ministry; and begin to work more to help mobilise churches around the whole country, to be more actively involved in mission work. We were moving to Chisinau, the capital city. OM's ministry was about to really take off; and not only our team, but also our family, was about to experience significant growth.

CHAPTER FIFTEEN

A Fleece Goes Hoop, Hoop!

It was the spring of 2001. I was at the vet's trying to hold a drip into her vein whilst *Honey,* our German Shepherd guard dog, looked at me with big, scared eyes and tried to squirm off the treatment table. A bulge formed under her skin and grew bigger and bigger. I guessed the antibiotic drip was not flowing where it should flow, but I had no idea what to do. After some time, the vet returned and shouted at me in Russian. He seemed angry with me – obviously I was doing it all wrong, which I thought was rather harsh as I never claimed to be a vet's assistant! The vet impatiently finished administering the medicine and then explained, this time in Moldovan, that the dog was very sick and that I should give her a *'clisma'* when I got home! I was afraid of dogs – having been bitten as a child – and I really didn't want to own a dog. It was just that we had moved to Chisinau, the capital city and we needed a guard dog and so we had bought Honey. I was afraid of her, but she was ill and I had little choice. I had taken her to the vets and been left holding her down whilst trying to hold a needle, in her leg, at the right angle so as to administer the antibiotics. I asked what the prognosis was – the vet helpfully informed me that Honey would either live or she would die!

During our three years living in Moldova, I had learnt that missionary life involved so much more than just feeling spiritual, studying and preaching. Since I had been serving on the mission field, I had learnt about auto-mechanics, fixed vehicles with duct tape and wire coat hangers, transported a cow in the team van[21], moved flea-ridden furniture between villages and even dead bodies from the market-place to the morgue. I had carried tons of water, and chatted to people at the spring, played football and tried to share my faith with the young and old, organised and run camps for children, learnt about budgeting and book-keeping, importing and exporting, visited the elderly, distributed humanitarian supplies, raised finances for different projects, established small businesses to provide work for people, as well as preached, evangelised, discipled and taught people from God's Word. I had learnt that the missionary life was diverse and consisted of many challenges and new experiences – but it wasn't until I got home and looked up *'clisma'* in my Romanian/English dictionary that I drew the line – I decided that *this* missionary was definitely not going to try and do that to a dog![22]

On the 7th July 2000, a sister from the church in Nisporeni shared with Helen a verse from the book of Isaiah. She said God had placed this word on her heart for us.

Sing, barren woman,
  you who never bore a child;
burst into song, shout for joy,

21 A long story … we were just trying to help a poor family transport a cow 40 km. The cow got scared, lifted her tail and let's just say that our van was never quite the same again.
22 'Clisma' is Romanian for enema. Whilst our trusty book 'Where there is no doctor' had some helpful pictures of buckets of warm water and a hose pipe, I was not willing to risk my life by trying to administer this to a German Shepherd. Anyway, Honey soon made a full recovery but was never a good guard dog and was herself stolen within weeks.

you who were never in labour; …
Enlarge the place of your tent,
 stretch your tent curtains wide,
 do not hold back;
lengthen your cords,
 strengthen your stakes.
Isaiah 54:1a and 2

Within days of receiving this verse we were thrilled to discover that Helen was expecting. Despite her really struggling through that summer and often feeling very ill, we held on to the promise that we felt God had given us through this verse. God had blessed us, we were going to start a family, we began 'enlarging our tent', but never imagined then, just how large our 'tent' was going to have to become!

Whilst Helen was heavily pregnant, we moved from Nisporeni to Chisinau. We had bought a large house, in Schinoasa, on the outskirts of the city, which was to become the new OM head-quarters. God had provided all the funds, through generous do-nations, for purchasing and renovating the three-storey house. Overseeing our first ever building project proved to be a steep learning curve – but after six months of work we moved in. We had a small apartment built on the top floor and spent a few weeks settling in before we headed back to England for our bi-an-nual home assignment. The last months of 2000 were incredi-bly challenging as we continued living in Nisporeni but had to spend a lot of time travelling to Chisinau to oversee the renova-tion of the new OM centre. I found myself acting as architect, foreman and employer as I tried to co-ordinate builders, elec-tricians, plumbers, painters, plasterers and installers of heating systems amongst others. The young people from Nisporeni would sometimes travel with us and earn some money by helping out with the project. By the end of the year we were just about ready to move in. Marianne from Switzerland, and Snejana from the church in Nisporeni, joined our team in Chisinau, whilst Rafael and Alis, missionaries from Romania, remained in Nisporeni and led the small team there.

We had a run-in with the local 'mafia' after first moving to Chisinau. A 'business man' visited us and demanded that we declare our income and pay taxes to him and his associates. We told him that all we had belonged to the Lord and that we spent all the money we had taking care of poor children and people like his grandmother in remote villages – so we had no extra money to 'declare'. We were left alone after that.

Helen surprised family and friends by arriving at Heathrow airport well into her seventh month pregnant, having not told anyone in England that we were expecting. Our beautiful baby, Hanna Olesea was born on 2nd February 2001 after a long and complicated delivery. Hanna must have been very comfortable in her mummy's tummy as she decided that she did not really want to be born at all and she got stuck. A specialist had to rush to Bournemouth hospital from another town to help with the delivery which was particularly traumatic. A few days after the birth, I wondered out loud if I could possibly go through such an ordeal again – Helen gave me one of her looks!

It was the most extraordinary experience to become a father for the first time. As I held little Hanna and looked at Helen, I did wonder whether it was sensible to take them back to Moldova. Wouldn't it be so much safer and easier just to settle in England? However, we knew that God had called us to Moldova – that our ministry there was only just beginning, so we drove the four-and-a-half day, three thousand kilometre journey, back from England to Moldova, with little Hanna safely tucked up in her car seat. Once again we experienced God providing for us. When we left England, we were driving our own car for the first time. We knew the safest place for our family was not in England but in the very centre of God's will – we and little Hanna were in His hands.

Over the next years, as we continued to lead the OM ministry in Moldova, we were blessed to see not only our team, but also our family grow. Lydia Marioara was born in 2002, Rachel Aliona in 2004, David Timothy in 2006 and James Thomas in 2007 – giving us five children under seven years old! The word from Isaiah 54, that had been shared with us, had really come true. Our tent had truly enlarged – and we told the sisters in Nisporeni to *please* stop praying for us!

The challenges and blessings of raising five children on the mission field would fill a whole other book. Suffice it to say for now, it has not always been easy, – especially for Helen – but God's grace and strength have been sufficient. Our home is always full of noise, laughter, fun, energy and the occasional tears.

––––––––––

It was during our first year living in Nisporeni, that we visited Ria and her family. Ria had made a profession of faith and was attending the church. One foggy Saturday evening, we followed the instructions we had been given, and walked along a narrow, muddy path until we came to a small, run-down house. We pushed against the gate and followed the path to the front door, avoiding a skinny, yappy dog, which tried to be brave, but was really very scared. We entered the small kitchen which contained a table, two chairs and a broken bed in which Ria and her two children slept. Ria's mother-in-law slept on a dirty, moth-eaten couch in the same room. We sat at the table and in the light of a homemade wax candle we talked with the family about life and faith. I couldn't help feeling that I was visiting a home from the middle-ages. There was no electricity, gas or running water. The only heat emanated from the small, make-shift oven, that was fuelled by wood scavenged from the forest.

As we were leaving, I glanced into an adjacent room that clearly was not in use. I saw that the room only had floorboards covering half of the floor. Ria was embarrassed and tried to close the door quickly as she explained, almost apologetically, that a couple of weeks earlier her father had died. She had no money to buy a coffin and so she had taken the floorboards up, built a coffin and buried her father!

Helen and I returned to our small apartment in the centre of town and we could barely speak. We knew that Ria's family was one of thousands upon thousands in Moldova who were living in abject poverty. We were beginning to see and experience something of the incredible needs of the people, and we wondered almost hopelessly, what we possibly could do to make a difference. I reflected upon the words of the song that has so touched my heart years earlier …

"I want to live my life for something that will last forever …"

We wanted to make a difference, we wanted to do something, but what could we do when there were *so* many needs, when there was *so* much suffering all around us?

We believed in sharing our faith and proclaiming the Good News; however, if practical actions did not accompany our words, then were we really doing everything that God was calling us to do? We knew that Jesus was concerned for people's physical and emotional, as well as spiritual needs, and we realised that any ministry that we were to be involved in, in Moldova, needed to reflect this holistic approach to the Gospel.

And so, in those early months living in Moldova, the relief and development ministries of OM Moldova were born. Over subsequent years, we imported many loads of humanitarian goods, which were distributed, through churches, to the poorest people in communities. We never knew then, that over the next decade, this would develop into a truly national ministry, mobilising Christians to work closely with local authorities in dozens of villages, daily feeding and caring for hundreds of children and elderly people, whilst also providing food, clothes and wood for thousands of others each winter.[23] Many people have been helped, and lives truly transformed, as we have tried to demonstrate God's love through OM's relief ministries. However, we always try to remember that all of those people are individuals, who, just like Ria, live with extraordinary needs that only God can truly meet.

We were thrilled to see the beginnings of this holistic approach to OM Moldova's mission work in Nisporeni, but realised that we couldn't be involved *only* in humanitarian relief. To make a real difference, we surely should seek to establish development projects to help bring about a long-term transformation in communities. So, we worked closely with churches around the country, helping to provide humanitarian aid for the poorest people – but also beginning projects that would help people to work and provide for themselves. In the early years in Nisporeni, we provided employment for people by starting sewing, woodworking and shoe repair shops – as well as various agricultural projects that provided work for people in the community. Over the next decade, God sent us wonderful gifted people who helped us further develop this ministry. We wanted OM Moldova to become more indigenously led; and were thrilled when Moldovans took over leading these departments and continued to develop the ministry of Business for Transformation (B4T). This ministry has since helped more than four hundred families

23 By 2014 OM Moldova was working with twenty churches, feeding and educating four hundred children each day. Another twenty churches were caring for and feeding some three hundred elderly people whilst a further 200 churches are mobilised to reach out to 2000 poor families each winter through various relief and development projects.

begin small businesses and therefore not have to leave the country to seek employment.

I never dreamt that missionary life would be so challenging and diverse. I found myself having to learn about, and oversee, relief and community development projects – as well as having to understand and administer business plans, raise money, and approve loans, for people who wanted to make a future for themselves by starting small businesses.[24]

In a similar way, literature and sports ministries, as well as summer camps and satellite local outreach teams, all had their beginnings in our ministry in Nisporeni in those early years. It was there that we first glimpsed the needs and also possibilities for helping churches to be mobilised in order to reach out more effectively to the needy in their communities. Whilst we were encouraged and excited about how the relief, development, business, sports and literature work was developing, it was however, our national missions training programme that was to have the biggest impact and become the heartbeat and centrepiece of OM Moldova over the following years.

———————

Ever since we joined OM, we have always taken one day each month – as a day away from work – to fast, pray and seek God's direction for our lives and the ministry. This has always been an extremely important day in our calendar and much of the strength of our ministry in Moldova finds its roots in this important prayer time each month. So it was that one spring day in 1999, Helen and I, with our small team, walked up the hill that overlooks Nisporeni to pray for the town and seek God about

24 By 2014 more than 400 families had received a loan to start businesses and hundreds more had received training in starting businesses which demonstrate 'kingdom values'.

the work we were involved in. We understood that if we really wanted to be effective and make a difference, then our calling was not just to come to Moldova as foreigners and 'do ministry', but rather we should seek to work alongside existing churches, help to mobilise them to be more active in reaching out and fulfil their part in the Great Commission. It was with this in mind that our team spent the day praying for Nisporeni and Moldova, trying to listen to what God was saying to us.

I went for a walk and was interested to come across a pair of strange looking birds hopping around under the trees. I recognised them immediately. A few years earlier, Helen and I had been travelling through Hungary when she loudly exclaimed "Look, did you see that?" We were nowhere near Nuremberg so I wondered what she was shouting about. She *claimed* to have seen a bird the size of a small chicken with a long curved beak, orange chest, black and white wings, and to top it all, a prominent orange crest. I made fun of Helen's imagination all the way back to our apartment in Austria, but she was adamant that she had seen a strange new bird. On arriving home and looking through a book of birds, she pointed triumphantly to a bird called a hoopoe and claimed that this was what she had seen. I knew little about hoopoes – other than they were designated as 'unclean' in the Bible – you see I really had read through Leviticus! I was rather sceptical of Helen's claim, but over the next years we always kept our eyes open for Helen's hoopoes and managed to see a few each summer. It has become a competition between us over the years as to who can see the first hoopoe of the year.

So it was, on that specific prayer day, that I sat and watched a pair of hoopoes flying around like big butterflies and rooting around on the ground for bugs or worms. As I sat and watched them, I thought about our calling to be missionaries in Moldova and sensed that God was speaking to us about starting something new. I returned to Helen and the team. As we discussed and prayed, we came up with the idea of a ten-week mission training course for young people. It would be a practical mission programme, designed to help mobilise Christians to be more active in reaching out to people by sharing and demonstrating their faith. The idea for OM Moldova's 'Challenge into Missions' (CiM) was born. By that autumn we had planned the first pilot-programme, where we would recruit a group of young people to be trained and mobilised to work with churches throughout the country.

We started to spread the word in Nisporeni and beyond, and had a group of around twenty young people recruited for the first programme. Some friends from another mission which worked amongst students (IFES), shared with us that they knew of a young man who was interested in joining our missions training course. This young man had been kicked out of his home because of his faith in Jesus. His parents had stopped supporting his university studies and he had been found sleeping rough in the park in Chisinau. I went to meet the young man and as soon as I saw him I recognised him. It was Mihai who we had met in a college in Cahul three years earlier! It was the most incredible coincidence. In fact we knew it was more than a coincidence. Only God could have arranged such a meeting three years after first sharing with this young man, in a different city and praying that he would come to faith. Mihai told us his story. He shared how after we had met in 1996, he had begun to study the Bible and had come to faith. However, on returning to his home village he had been rejected by his father because of his faith and now he had nowhere to stay. We were thrilled to have Mihai join the training and then travel with our teams for the next weeks sharing the Gospel. After that outreach it was wonderful to see how Mihai was baptised, joined OM and became the first Moldovan to work full-time with us. Mihai joined our team and helped us pioneer OM Moldova's literature ministry, whilst also subsidising his missionary support through book sales. The literature ministry was later to grow into a national ministry. Now we see Christian books, and especially Bibles, going to the furthest corners of the country, taken out by evangelistic teams and the *Bus4Life* – a mobile bookshop and outreach centre, that travels around the country a few times each year.

The first full Challenge into Missions course began in our apartment in Nisporeni in the spring of 2000, with seven recruits. The ten-week programme consisted of four weeks of practical studies and six weeks of working with churches around the country, where students put into practice the things that had been learnt. Rafael and Alis were part of the first CiM, as was Tamara who had continued on in her new faith since praying with us in 1996 – she was keen to learn more about becoming a missionary and serving God.[25] Challenge into Missions has run twice, each year, ever since its humble beginnings in our apartment in 2000. By 2010 we had celebrated a jubilee of twenty programmes in ten years. By 2015, some six-hundred Christians had graduated from the missions training course and gone on to serve as missionaries with OM, or returned to serve the Lord in their home churches. We increasingly understood that as foreign missionaries, our calling, and the best use of our time, was to invest in local Christians – to help to mobilise others to reach out rather than just us doing it ourselves. And it all began with a day of prayer and fasting, two hoopoes, a vision and a willingness to take a risk and start something new.

---

25 We had quite miraculously bumped into Tamara again about one year after her conversion in 1996. Whilst driving to the south we had come across a young lady hitch-hiking with a leg of a pig sticking out of her bag. We slowed at the strange sight and recognised immediately Tamara and gave her a lift into the local town. The Lord seemed to have a plan and purpose for us as we continued to meet her on our subsequent trips to Moldova.

In the early 2000s, with us now based in Chisinau, the ministry of OM continued to grow and develop as we partnered with churches throughout the whole country. As we placed increasing emphasis on recruiting for, and running the CiM programme, we saw as a knock-on effect, more people recruited to join our team(s). With all the new recruits joining OM, we were able to see further growth in the ministries of relief, community development, B4T, Sports and Youth, Bus Ministry (Bus4Life) as well as short-term mission outreaches and of course the central Challenge into Missions course.

Our vision for ministry had always been to mobilise people from around the world to help local churches to be more active in reaching out to the lost. Within a decade of moving to Chisinau and establishing a national, rather than just localised ministry, we had over fifty full-time workers serving with OM Moldova and hundreds more joining us for short term outreaches and training programmes each year.

Our vision statement emphasises OM's desire to help churches reach out locally as well as internationally:

OM exists in Moldova to help place mission at the heart of the Church and the Church at the heart of the community.

As I began to travel more extensively around Moldova, I spoke more and more not only of the needs to be active in local missions, but also to be aware of the incredible needs for the truths of the Gospel to be proclaimed and demonstrated in other countries. Even though the church in Moldova is, relatively speaking small,[26] our vision was to see missionaries raised up and sent out to some of the lesser reached countries in the world. Mihai was the first Moldovan missionary to be sent out internationally through OM as he served in Nepal for a year. After Mihai

26 There are around forty thousand Evangelical church members in Moldova, around 1% of the population.

we saw dozens of Moldovans mobilised and sent out by their churches to serve in some of the least reached countries of central Asia, North Africa the Middle East and Balkans, as well as serving on the OM ships.

We continued to face significant problems and challenges after moving from Nisporeni to Chisinau. Certainly the living conditions became easier – as did communications with the outside world – yet as the ministry grew, and OM Moldova gained a higher profile, so the challenges grew. I could write more about negotiations with dodgy businessmen, local priests and even neighbours who threatened our lives. I could write about being refused re-entry into the country in 2006, days of medical tests to gain approval for residency permits, team-members being deported, robbed, going missing and even dying. I could write about being stopped by the police on a hill in Chisinau, taken from the van to check papers and then watching as my van took off on its own and ploughed into the side of a police car. I could write of a hundred other challenging situations; yet amongst the most difficult has always been trying to provide leadership for other missionaries and work with other Christians.

There have certainly been many discouraging and challenging moments during our 'Missionary adventure' but we have never even toyed with the idea of just giving up. It is when those 'wonderful' brothers or sisters – who seem to specialise in a ministry of discouragement appear – that I find myself thinking of the little boy stranded alone on the goal line, the ball stuck between his knees – and everyone staring.

When people criticise and attack, it can be easy to become discouraged, be tempted to give up and refuse to play football again. However, I believe the challenge is always to try to ignore the critics, roll up my sleeves and get on with what I feel the Lord has called me to do.

I continue to be challenged and encouraged by the words that struck me so profoundly in the jungle of Guyana.

I'll obey and serve you
I'll obey because I love you,
I'll obey my life is in your hands
For it's the way to prove my life
When feelings go away
And if it costs me everything
I'll obey [27]

There have been testing and challenging times, but there have also been so many reminders over the years, showing and reassuring us that God has called us *to* and blessed us *in* this ministry in Moldova. It has been such a privilege to see first-hand how He works, transforming lives and communities over the years.

In moments of doubt or discouragement, I just have to think about the little church in Micleuseni that we helped to plant in the 1990s. The church now has a couple of dozen members, an active children's and youth work, has sent young people who used to be in Helen's Sunday School class to our CiM training, has an ordained deacon and is itself now planting two other churches in surrounding villages. I think of the missionaries who have been raised up from Nisporeni and still serve with us, fulfilling key ministries in OM Moldova. [28] I think of the many Moldovans who have served with OM overseas, amongst whom have been three from Pavel's church in Ciniseuti who served in central Asia,

---

27 "I'll Obey" By Jim Custer, Tim Hosman © 1983 C.A. Music and sung by Bill Drake, OM Arts International

28 Tudor for example served for two years in a closed country. Spiridon who came to faith through the first summer camp we ran in Nisporeni in 1999 is now leader of one of OM's local ministry teams. Snejana who joined OM from the church in Nisporeni in 2001, served with OM in Albania for a couple of years and has since become one of the senior leaders within OM Moldova and heads up Human Resources and Mobilising departments.

whilst dozens of others have trained with us, continue to serve with OM and have taken on leading roles within and outside Moldova.

I think also of Tamara who came to faith on our outreach to Cahul 1996. We kept in touch with her and visited her as she grew in her faith over the following years. Tamara returned to her village Paicu, near Cahul, after finishing high-school, as the only believer and began leading people to faith. After completing her Missions Training with us, Tamara became one of the first Moldovans to join OM full-time. For more than a decade she led one of OM's local ministry teams in her home village, where a church has been established, and dozens have come to faith. OM's relief, development and B4T projects help place the church at the heart of the community – as believers are equipped to reach out to people in the village – and over the years thousands have been touched by the love of God. The church in Paicu is now also planting churches in other villages. The believers understand that just as they have been blessed, and have experienced transformed lives through the working of God's Holy Spirit, so they also are called to share that blessing and Good News with others.

Just as my life was turned upside down after a mission trip to Estonia in 1992, we sometimes hear from people who served with us in Moldova at some stage over the years, and also went through a life changing experience. It is so encouraging to hear how God has used the ministry in Moldova to open people's eyes to the needs in the world; and it is wonderful to hear of people who took their first steps in mission in Moldova and are now serving the Lord in countries like Russia, Ukraine, Haiti, Indonesia, Romania, Brazil and beyond. Many more have returned home, motivated and encouraged to be more actively involved in serving God, having first tasted missions in Moldova.

We still enjoy the occasional visit to the 'golden arches' of McDonalds, but nowadays use the children as an excuse to go and eat unhealthy food. On one visit in 2009, a young man approached Helen and said that he recognised her. He asked if I was around and approached the table where I was sitting, with a big smile on his face. I recognised Serghei from Cahul immediately even though I had not seen him for around fifteen years. Serghei shared his story. He described how after meeting us, and hearing the Gospel for the first time, he had travelled around Europe, searching for work and purpose in life. He said that despite many problems, difficulties and getting involved with the wrong crowd, he always remembered the words of hope that we had shared with him in the market-place in Cahul all those years earlier. God's Word had been sown in his heart and after many years on the run, Serghei was deported back to Moldova, where he finally made a life-changing decision to follow Jesus Christ. As we talked outside McDonalds, Serghei shared how he was now a member of a church in the south, and actually was in Chisinau with his youth group – which he now led! I silently whispered a prayer of thanks to God. He had called us to this ministry and we considered it such a privilege to glimpse, occasionally, the fruits of our service. God reminded me, through Serghei, that it was worth it – the tiredness, the upset stomachs, the stress, the cold, the travelling, the loneliness – missing family and friends, the break-downs, the injections, the financial challenges, even the cabbage! It *was* worth it – it *is* worth it!

As the rain and the snow come down from heaven, and do not return to it without watering the earth and making it bud and flourish, so that it yields seed for the sower and bread for the eater, so is my word that goes out from my mouth: It will not return to me empty, but will accomplish what I desire and achieve the purpose for which I sent it. (Isaiah 55:10–11)

Now, as I look back at more than two decades of serving on the mission field, I realise just how much God has transformed me during these years. Did I really used to think that believing in God and the Christian faith was somehow irrelevant to my life and my plans for my future? Did I really used to think that God was kind of distant and uninterested in me? Did I really used to think that Christians lived boring lives, and doubt the validity of Jesus' claim that true life, abundant life was found only when living in relationship with Him?

When Helen and I first returned to Moldova in 2001, with our new-born baby, Hanna, there was a sense of uncertainty. It was one thing setting off on the mission field as a single guy, wanting adventure and not afraid to swim with crocodiles. It was another step heading off with a wife and having to trust God to provide for and protect us as a couple. But now, I was heading back to Moldova with a wife *and* new-born baby?! In addition, we were returning not to our home in Nisporeni but to the capital city Chisinau, with questions and uncertainties about our future and the national ministry we sensed God was calling us to.

On Saturday 20th May 2001 we had the inauguration and opening of the new OM office and training centre in Chisinau. It was a wonderful step in the development of the ministry in Moldova – but within days I had become discouraged. I really had enjoyed living and ministering in Nisporeni and now, here we were in Chisinau, in some ways having to start again, as we prepared to try and build a national ministry. On Friday 25th I took a day to pray, fast and seek God. I wrote in my journal and questioned God …

"Are you really in this? Did you really want us to buy this house as a mission centre for OM – shouldn't we be back in Nisporeni? Is this all really of you Lord?"

As I prayed and wrote these questions, I felt His presence in a special way, and 'heard' Him speak. Now you could argue that it was just my imagination fuelled by hunger from fasting, but I was sure that the Lord was present, once again, in a special way. I am sure that the increasingly familiar Voice asked – *"What sign shall I give you?"* I had read about Gideon 'putting out a fleece' and King Hezekiah asking for the shadow on the steps to go backwards rather than forwards – but I did not really feel comfortable to ask God for such a sign. Those sort of things were for Old Testament prophets and kings. It did not really fit my theology to ask for a sign – surely I was just allowing my imagination to run a bit too wild!? As I looked out of the window, I saw some sparrows sitting on the corner of our roof. Then it came to my mind and I spoke to God, "If I could just see a hoopoe today, then I would take that as a sign that *you* have called us to this ministry in Chisinau!" There it was, I had said it! I knew that unless I went for a drive in the forest, the chances of God answering this request were remote. We lived on the third floor of a house in a residential area, on the outskirts of Chisinau. I was just being silly, imagining voices and conversations with God – maybe I was going mad! What had happened to me? I had become one of those ridiculous, 'over-spiritual', weird Christians that I had grown up trying to avoid. Perhaps it was time to return to England, raise my family there and just live a 'normal' life. As I walked from the living room to the kitchen I was even more discouraged and fed up – some *quality*, quiet time with the Lord that had been – what a waste of time, imagining voices and daydreaming!

Then I heard it …

Hoop, hoop, hoop!

I walked through the kitchen to the dining area and looked out of the glass door leading to the balcony. *Hoop, hoop, hoop!* I could not believe my ears and my eyes. There it was, a funny-looking bird with an orange chest, black and white wings, a long beak and orange crest. A hoopoe was perched on the TV aerial on the top of our house, just three metres from where I was standing. "Hoop, hoop, hoop" he said, which when translated from hoop-ese means, *"Matthew do you believe me now?"*

I stood there, amazed, and I knew, I just knew. This was no coincidence!

I never saw another hoopoe in that area of the city again. But there it had been, on that day, and as I stood there and reflected on how stupid I was for doubting God, once again I sensed that He was smiling.

Now, every time I see a hoopoe, I think of God's goodness and the confirmation of His calling on my life. I think of a young teenager who was confused and ashamed of the Gospel and the Christian faith. I think of a young man who wanted to live a fun-loving, exciting life but never thought that this 'fullness of life' could really be found as a follower of Jesus Christ. I think of God's incredible, and sometimes miraculous provision. I think of travel and love, crocodiles and soldiers, life and death, ships and illness, blessing and provision, ugly angels and the KGB, Dracula's castle and holy kisses and miracles, answered prayers and a girl and a Voice and a call. I think of my parents, my brother, my wife, my children and our faithful supporters – and I am filled with thanksgiving and I stand in awe at what God has done.

I am learning that maybe it is possible to live my life for something that will last forever.

Missionary, me?!

Disturb us, Lord, when
We are too pleased with ourselves,
When our dreams have come true
Because we dreamed too little,
When we arrived safely
Because we sailed too close to the shore.

Disturb us, Lord, when
With the abundance of things we possess
We have lost our thirst
For the waters of life;
Having fallen in love with life,
We have ceased to dream of eternity
And in our efforts to build a new earth,
We have allowed our vision
Of the new Heaven to dim.

Disturb us, Lord, to dare more boldly,
To venture on wilder seas
Where storms will show Your mastery;
Where losing sight of land,
We shall find the stars.

We ask you to push back
The horizons of our hopes;
And to push back the future
In strength, courage, hope, and love.

This we ask in the name of our Captain,
Who is Jesus Christ.

Sir Francis Drake 1577

Epilogue

More than a quarter of a century has passed since I tried to impress a girl by reading my Bible and going on a mission trip. (Am I really that old?) I recognise how much I have changed since those teenage years, how much God has changed and moulded me, and how He is still at work transforming me into the person He wants me to become. I often whisper a prayer of thanks as I acknowledge how He has taken me by the hand and led me through these years. I have experienced His faithfulness, protection and blessing and seen answered prayers, sometimes in quite extraordinary ways, whilst visiting more than fifty countries on my missionary journey so far. Christians – "Boring people, boring lives!" … did I really use to think that?

———————

I look back to our early impressions of Moldova from the mid-1990s, and consider the changes that have taken place in the country since then. Certainly, there has been some economic growth and development, yet still there are people who are desperately poor and needing to hear and experience the truths of the Gospel. One significant change we have seen is that the population has fallen in twenty years from four-and-a-half million, when we first visited, to closer to three-and-a-half million today.

This significant decrease in population is largely due to the emigration of people who seek work in other countries and have left to try and build a better future abroad.

The Evangelical church has also faced unique challenges having seen spectacular growth in the 1990s. By 2008 the growth had plateaued and whilst people are still coming to faith, these days, an equal number continue to leave the church or emigrate. As OM, we continue to work with all Evangelical churches in the country helping believers reach out into their communities and beyond.

———————

We truly love Moldova and the Moldovan people. Our time spent in this beautiful, but sometimes troubled, country has left an indelible mark on our lives and we thank God for the rich experience and privilege that it has been to raise our family in Moldova and grow up there together.

One of the most rewarding aspects of raising our family on the mission field has been having the possibility to involve our children in ministry, as we have visited and reached out together to the poor and needy. I continue to see how God uses my natural desire for adventure and pioneering spirit in mission work, and we are always looking for new ways to motivate and equip Christians to be active in reaching out, demonstrating and sharing God's love with as many people as possible. In 2010, for example, recognising that very little was being done to reach the villages in the north-east of Moldova where there are no Evangelical churches, we developed special "river outreaches". It is exciting every summer when we prepare and send out teams of Christians to sail down the Nistru River, on home-made rafts, seeking to share the Good News to people in unreached villages.

By 2014 the OM team had grown to over sixty missionaries serving full time and many more employed in projects with churches around the country. The leadership team was made up of myself and four very capable and competent Moldovan Christians and I began to realise that our work, what God had called me and Helen to do in Moldova, was coming to an end. We started to sense that maybe God was calling us to a new challenge and that it was time for us to step aside and encourage others to take the ministry on in new ways. In the Spring of 2015 I was able to hand over the field leadership of OM Moldova to Eugen, a young Moldovan man and good friend, who had joined our Challenge into Missions programme in 2006 and worked alongside us for nine years.

As we stepped out of leadership it felt like we had, over the years, conceived, given birth to and raised a child. The child had needed much care and attention at the beginning, had gone through various stages of growth (including occasional difficult "teenage" years), but, by 2015 there was a sense that OM Moldova was no longer a child; the work had reached a level of maturity and was ready to become independent of us. We felt very much at peace, that it was the right time for the ministry, the team, and for us personally to move on. By God's grace something had been established, grown and developed that we believe can continue to make a difference in Moldova for many years.

How are you supposed to feel when handing over leadership of a ministry after twenty years? – Relief? Fulfilment? Happiness? Pride? (Oops shouldn't really admit that – should I?) Satisfaction? Bereavement? Maybe all of the above?!

As I took time to reflect upon (and recover from) two decades of pioneering and leading OM's ministry in Moldova, perhaps my overriding feeling was one of awe. It has been exciting, rewarding, challenging, often exhausting – but at the same time awesome to have seen and experienced God at work transforming lives – not least our own. *"To God be the glory great things HE has done."*

After handing over leadership of OM Moldova, in June of 2015, exactly twenty years after our first trip to Moldova, we sensed that ever more familiar voice whispering in our hearts and saying; *"I have called you to be missionaries, to serve me, to follow me. It is wonderful what has happened in Moldova, but now it is time to let go, it is time to move on, I have something else for you to do!"*

In the summer of 2015, with a step of faith at least as big as the one we took when we first headed to Moldova, we moved back to the UK – or maybe it would be better to say that we moved to the UK! It did not so much feel like moving back, or returning to our home country, as it was like entering a new country as missionaries for the first time. After all, the children had never lived in England and in many ways felt more Moldovan than English. So much had changed in the years since we had been students in London, but most significantly we had changed!

Since the autumn of 2015 we have been based in Shropshire, England. For some years I continued to minister in Eastern Europe serving as a Regional Leader for OM Europe, advising and overseeing OM's ministries in Romania and Moldova. One of my greatest joys in ministry has been to see how Eugen has provided such Godly and competent leadership for OM Moldova and seeing how God continues to lead and give wisdom, vision and innovative ideas as OM's work continues to flourish under his leadership.[29]

---

29 By 2018 the OM Moldova team had grown to more than seventy adults serving full time (twenty foreigners and fifty Moldovans). Not only the ministry continued to develop and be fruitful, but also many of the young people who had grown up with us have got married and an additional thirty plus children are also now part of the OM Moldova team – making us feel a little like Grandparents! God continues to bless and use OM Moldova to partner with churches in reaching out into local communities, least reached areas of the country and importantly, also sending out Moldovan missionaries to other countries.

In 2016 I was appointed as the new National Director for OM in the UK. When I first met the staff serving with OM UK I said, "I believe the same God who speaks Moldovan also speaks English." What I meant is that just as we have had the privilege of seeing and experiencing God at work in Moldova, transforming lives and communities, leading, guiding, protecting, providing for, blessing and answering all sorts of prayer – so I also believe that we can experience the same God working also in our new country of service.

Now we are based in the UK, our location has changed but we remain as committed as ever to the calling we believe the Lord has given us. We serve with OM, working in partnership with churches, seeking to see more people grow in awareness of mission needs around the world and in understanding how they (we) can be used by the Lord to make a difference and continue to fulfil His Great Commission. We remain as passionate as ever about helping to serve and mobilise Christians to be more actively involved in local, national and world missions. There are so many wonderful opportunities to serve with OM both short and long term – whether taking part in the amazing youth event TeenStreet, signing up for a summer outreach adventure, taking a Gap Year with OM, joining a Mission Discipleship Training program (MDT) or serving longer term as part of a mission team somewhere in the world, there are so many needs and exciting options! Please do check out our website at www.om.org or write to me if you would like more information about how you can get involved.

I often think back to the words of the song that so profoundly spoke to me at the OM Love Europe Conference in 1992. I still want to "live my life for something that will last forever" and I daily ask the Lord for strength, wisdom and grace to serve Him, to not waste my life but to make a difference for His Kingdom. There is still such an incredible need for the Gospel to be spread in our world. The Lord has called and indeed can use all of us who are willing to step out by faith and place our lives fully into His hands. The message then is that it is not just "Missionary, me!" But it can also be "Missionary, you!"

I wonder what story God may be calling you to write with your life?

I should add that after having such an influence in my life, Adam, my brother, went on to serve as a missionary in Uganda. He then trained as a teacher, studied theology and became a pastor. In 1997 he married Pip and now pastors a vibrant and growing church in the New Forest, in the south of England. He still encourages people to follow Jesus – and plays football regularly but still mistakenly thinks that he is better than me!

Finally, this is not meant to be a dull theological book, full of doctrines and boring stuff. It is simply the story of how God transformed my life, protected and provided for me and at times did some quite extraordinary things along the way. My prayer is that maybe, in some small way, this story of my life, my experiences and journey so far with God may encourage readers to (re)consider their own relationship with, and service for Him.

There may be things within this story that you question. That's okay. I still have lots of questions and often I simply do not understand why God works in certain ways. However, I believe that one day He will make everything clear. Until then we press on, knowing that He is in control, and understanding that He continues to call ordinary people to fulfil His extraordinary purposes.

Not that I have already obtained all this, or have already arrived at my goal, but I press on to take hold of that for which Christ Jesus took hold of me. Brethren, I do not regard myself as having laid hold of it yet; but one thing I do: forgetting what lies behind and reaching forward to what lies ahead, I press on toward the goal for the prize of the upward call of God in Christ Jesus (Philippians 3:12–14)

Appendix

What Does OM Do?

Working in every region of the world and on every ocean (via an ocean-going ship), Operation Mobilisation seeks to demonstrate and proclaim the love of God. In every situation OM teams adapt to the local culture and situation, finding the best ways to share Jesus' message.

Through literature, the creative arts, friendship, Bible studies, media, correspondence courses, relief and development work, business projects and much, much more we will tell people how our lives have been changed and how they also can meet Jesus.

Wherever possible, Operation Mobilisation works in partnership with the local church, encouraging and supporting local believers. Where there is no church we seek to plant churches.

Who We Are?

3 400 people working in over 110 countries are serving with Operation Mobilisation to bring a message of hope to the people of the world. Many more also join us for short term mission opportunities each year.

We have one thing in common – we love Jesus and we want others to have the opportunity to hear about Him.

Our Purpose

Operation Mobilisation works in more than 110 countries, motivating and equipping people to share God's love with people all over the world.

OM seeks to help plant and strengthen churches, especially in areas of the world where Christ is least known.

Our Vision

- Focusing on the unreached
- Partnering with churches
- Caring for our members
- Training and equipping world Christians
- Mobilising the next generation
- Globalising our ministry
- Strengthening our organisation

Our Core Values

- Knowing and glorifying God
- Living in submission to God's word
- Being people of grace and integrity
- Serving sacrificially
- Loving and valuing people
- Evangelising the world
- Reflecting the diversity of the body of Christ
- Global intercession
- Esteeming the Church

What We Believe

- We believe that there is one God, eternally existent in three persons, Father, Son and Holy Spirit.

- We believe in the absolute deity and full humanity of our Lord Jesus Christ. We believe in His virgin birth, His sinless life, the authenticity of His miracles, His vicarious and atoning death, His bodily resurrection and His present mediatorial work in heaven.

- We believe in the personality and deity of the Holy Spirit. We believe He gives life, He sanctifies, He empowers and comforts all believers.

- We believe that the Scriptures, both the Old and New Testaments in their original texts, are fully inspired by the Holy Spirit, without error, and are the final authority for the Church.

- We believe that man was originally created sinless. Tempted by Satan, man fell and thereby brought the whole race under the condemnation of eternal separation from God.

- We believe that man is saved through repentance and faith in the finished work of Christ. Justification is through grace alone.

- We believe that the Church is the body of Jesus Christ composed of all true believers. The present work of the Church is the worship of God, the perfecting of the saints and the evangelisation of the world.

- We believe in the personal and bodily return of the Lord Jesus Christ to consummate our salvation and establish His Glorious Kingdom.

Brief OM Timeline

1955 One woman prays
1957 George Verwer and friends make missionary trip to Mexico
1958 First Christmas Crusade in Mexico City
1960 Work begins in Spain
1962 First European Summer Outreach; long-term teams enter Middle East & North Africa
1963 Teams go to Israel & India
1966 Work begins in Communist Eastern Europe
1968 Work begins in Afghanistan & Nepal
1970 M.V. LOGOS ship is purchased
1972 Work begins in Bangladesh
1977 M.V. DOULOS ship is purchased
1980 Work begins in Pakistan
1988 M.V. LOGOS shipwrecked in South America – M.V. LOGOS II purchased
1989 LOVE EUROPE Summer Outreach begins with over 7 000 people. Hundreds join long-term.
1995 Work begins in Moldova
2002 Dalit Education Centres begin in India
2003 Peter Maiden appointed new International Director of OM
2004 LOGOS HOPE purchased
2009 Launch of OM ship Logos Hope
2013 Lawrence Tong appointed new International Director of OM
2015 Twenty-year Celebration of OM Moldova
2017 OM celebrates 60 years and launches new Mission Statement

We want to see vibrant communities of Jesus followers among the least reached

For more information about OM International visit
www.om.org (/md or /uk)